Front Stage, Backstage

Organization Studies
John Van Maanen, General editor

Front Stage, Backstage

The Dramatic Structure
of Labor Negotiations

Raymond A. Friedman

The MIT Press
Cambridge, Massachusetts
London, England

This book was set in Palatino by The MIT Press and was printed and bound in the United States of America.

Library of Congress Cataloging-in-Publication Data

Friedman, Raymond A. (Raymond Alan), 1958–
Front stage, backstage: the dramatic structure of labor negotiations / Raymond A. Friedman.
    p.   cm.—(MIT Press series on organization studies; 10)
Includes bibliographical references and index.
ISBN 0-262-06167-8
1. Collective bargaining. I. Title. II. Series.
HD6971.5.F75   1994
331.89—dc20   93-44591
                                                                    CIP

for Jen-Jen and Toni

Contents

Acknowledgments

Negotiations are times of great anxiety, pressure, hope, and fear for labor and management alike. Those who helped me gain access to their negotiations, tolerated by presence at the bargaining table, and answered my questions were taking a risk that I fully understood only in hindsight. I want first to thank all of these people, whose names I cannot list because of promises of confidentiality, for their willingness to take a risk and for the insights they brought to this study.

As with any research project many people influenced the ideas that are presented in this book and provided personal support and encouragement. This work began when I unexpectedly discovered in my study of International Harvester the passion with which negotiators talked about the process of negotiation, and their anger at deviations from what was expected. During the time I was trying to make sense of these observations, Edward Laumann, Wendy Griswold, and Paul Hirsch at the University of Chicago provided a sounding board for my interpretations and helped me to form them into a coherent story. Barbara Marsh shared generously the materials that she had collected for her book on International Harvester.

After my arrival at Harvard the scope of the research broadened, and I spent several years attending negotiations and talking to dozens of negotiators. As I presented my developing ideas in seminars and talked with colleagues about my research, I learned from the comments and criticisms of Richard Hackman, Michael Piore, Jay Lorsch, Richard Walton, Thomas Kochan, Shoshana Zuboff, Jim Sebenius, David Krackhardt, Anne Donnellon, Jack Gabarro, David Thomas, and Mike Gibbs. I am especially thankful for the advice, support, and feedback that both Charles Heckscher and Deborah Kolb provided throughout this project. It was Debbie who suggested that I take more seriously the drama analogy that was emerging in my writing, and it was Charles who made it possible for me to study the mutual gains cases. He was also the person who was always there to listen to the latest new idea. As I ventured into the territory of mutual gains bargaining, I joined a group of people who were also studying this topic, from whom I learned a great deal, including Robert McKersie, Larry Susskind, Jerry Barrett, Don Power, Joel Cutcher-Gershenfeld, Ed Herman, and Larry Hunter, as well as Charles Heckscher. Toward the end of the project, it was the careful readings of the manuscript by Peter Cappelli, Robert McKersie, Jane Gebhart, and, above all, John Van Maanen that enabled me to focus my writing. Finally, at MIT Press Terry Vaughn and Dana Andrus guided me through the final process of turning a manuscript into a book.

I was also fortunate to have had a great deal of help from many dedicated research assistants and support staff. Complete field observations would not have been possible without the hard work of Caitlin Deinard, who spent many hours attending negotiations with me, and Shahaf Gal, who both observed negotiations and collaborated on an early article that came from this project. Mike Stevenson provided ongoing library support, Philip Hamilton helped analyze statistical data, and Jennifer Wilson, Anne Brzoza, and the staff of the word-processing center provided capable secretarial support. Funding for this project was generously provided by Harvard Business School, and the research on International Harvester was made possible by a grant from the University of Chicago.

My thanks go out to all of those who contributed their ideas, research assistance, and moral support to the project. The most important moral support of all was that of my wife, Jen-Jen Lin, who tolerated the many ups and downs that come with a project like this, and would not allow me to lose touch with home and family.

Front Stage, Backstage

1   Introduction

The labor relations system in the United States has been under great pressure to change over the past decade. A system that had been lauded for providing stability and industrial peace in the 1960s and 1970s is now seen as bureaucratic and inefficient. Managers have become emboldened to confront or avoid unions as public and political support for them has weakened, and membership has declined.[1] Concerned observers of the labor movement have suggested that if unions are to survive, they have to radically rethink what services they provide to members

1. Claims about the ineffectiveness of the current labor-realtions system abound. McCormick (1985) writes: "Sheltered from foreign and major domestic competition, managers gave in to labor's wage demands and paid dividends to their shareholders; however, they failed to innovate and invest sufficiently in their companies. When the economic circumstances change, these patterns were no longer feasible . . . These patterns have outlived their usefulness and may have accelerated the decline of these industries by impeding their adaptation to a new competitive environment" (p. 142). And Weiler (1990) reports that "American industry has persuaded itself that the institution is far too ossified a mechanism with which to burden the enterprise in the more testing climate of the eighties and nineties" (p. 14). Lack of public confidence in unions is apparent from public polls (see Heckscher 1988, 53), and the decline of political support for unions was signaled clearly by President Ronald Reagan's dismissal of striking air traffic controllers in 1981. The fact that management is now willing to make strategic decisions about unions that include decertification campaigns, union avoidance, and protracted battles over wages and work rules is well documented by Kochan, Katz, and McKersie (1986) and Walton, Cutcher-Gershenfeld, and McKersie (forthcoming). And studies of the decline of union membership have become something of a mini-industry in academe (see, e.g., Goldfield 1987 or Fiorito 1991).

and how those services can be provided. And concerned observers of industry have suggested that if our major industries are
to survive, labor and management must become allies, not
adversaries.[2]

Despite these pressures for change, and the proliferation of
alternative visions of the future, change has been difficult.
Robert McKersie, one of the authors of an influential book that
predicted a "transformation" of American industrial relations,
commented recently (1991): "it must be admitted that the transformation of U.S. labor relations . . . has been proceeding much
more slowly than we had hoped or anticipated" (p. 2). Some
changes have occurred on the shop-floor level of the industrial
relations system; we often hear about quality initiatives, employee involvement, teamwork, and job restructuring. But the core of
the labor relations system—collective bargaining—seems especially resistant to change. Recent efforts to bring a win-win
approach to labor relations have proved extraordinarily difficult,
and past efforts to change the negotiation process, such as the
Human Relations committee in basic steel, have faded away.[3]

What can explain the persistence of an institution that has
been so roundly criticized by so many people? One might argue

2. Heckscher (1988), a careful observer of the union movement, argues that unions
should move toward a more "associational" form of organization in order to be more
flexible and effective: "effective representation requires employee organizations that
are, relative to current unions, more decentralized, have a greater ability to educate
members about complex issues, and can build unity around a general vision rather
than a fixed contract" (p. 177). And Dyer, Salter, and Webber (1987) argue that competition in the auto industry is no longer between U.S. companies but between the
industrial enterprise systems of the United States and Japan. While the later system
is built on cooperation between labor and management, the U.S. system, "dating
back to the early 1950's, called for management to insist on control of the work place
and the union to wrest economic rewards from management on behalf of the workers" (p. 236). If U.S. industry is going to compete with Japan, management must
develop a more cooperative relationship with labor. In terms of competitiveness,
these authors say, "the old relationship is obsolete" (p. 236).
3. Reports on the difficulties negotiators have had with mutual gains bargaining are
found in Heckscher (1993), Friedman (1992a, 1993a), Cutcher-Gershenfeld (1993),
and Hunter and McKersie (1992). Heckscher (1993), includes a discussion of past
efforts to change labor negotiations.

that labor and management negotiators are blind to the changes that have occurred. But that is unlikely. Most people in labor relations can see all too well the pressures they face. One might also argue that they see what is happening but then proceed to act in traditional ways because they are habit bound and irrational. It is probably true that more than a few negotiators are irrational and habit bound, but it is unlikely that individual deficiencies of this type are the cause of a pattern of behavior that is widespread. A completely different answer, and the one that is developed in this book, is that the traditional negotiation process *makes sense*. Many books have been written recently about the "new" industrial relations system—this book is about the logic of the old one.

The traditional negotiation process represents an institutionalized pattern of behavior that helps negotiators respond sensibly to the demands placed on them. It enables negotiators to manage constituent pressures, maintain their group identity, and act as leaders of a team. In order to understand the rituals of bargaining and their persistence, we must examine, not just the logic of strategic moves but also the motives and behaviors of negotiators as they act within a social context. The study of negotiations is currently dominated by theories of individual rationality or irrationality; a more full and realistic understanding of the labor negotiation process (or any negotiations that include large groups, political pressure, and constituent observation) requires a theory of the *social* structure of negotiations.

The Typical Process

What, exactly, is the "traditional" process of negotiation whose persistence has to be explained? While no two negotiations are exactly the same, there is pattern of behavior that is known and expected by experienced negotiators. As a local union president at International Harvester put it: "There was a formula for it. It's no big secret." A labor relations manager at the same company pointed out:

> The script was written and you could just about predict what was going to be said, what the union's list would look like, what our list would look like, how meetings would go, and how the adjournments would happen.

Based on my field research, this "script" begins with each side collecting its thoughts and rallying its troops. Often the union reminds members of management's past deeds—their own management's or management in general. Both sides set goals and objectives and develop a bargaining strategy. Then, in the first meetings, each side presents an exhaustive list of changes that it would like, called a "laundry list," and broadly explains the requests. The company says that it needs to be competitive and cannot afford much more; the union explains that its members are angry and demand just treatment. After these preliminary steps, negotiations begin in earnest. At first the negotiators stand tough. Then slowly each side signals what it really cares about by expressing their rejections in softer or harder terms, and mentioning their own proposals more or less often. Stock phrases, with well-known meanings, are used to indicate where they really stand. Some issues just "fall off the table" and are forgotten. There is some horse trading, as proposals from each side are simultaneously accepted or dropped.

Throughout this process the conversations across the table are usually brisk and contentious, and the mood is one of anger and apprehension. Negotiators are careful to say only what is planned and reveal only what they must: They rarely admit that the other side has a good point. The lead bargainer usually coaches his or her teams on what to say and when to say it, and when negotiators do improvise, they still maintain their roles—their comments display anger and distrust toward the opponent, as well as solidarity with their teammates. Negotiators rarely let down their guard during negotiations: Both their words and their attitude are highly controlled.

During caucuses negotiators try to discern their opponent's true position and to clarify any disagreements on their own goals. The lead bargainer stands apart from the others, showing that he or she knows what the opponents really meant by their last move, and what the team should do in response. In many cases he or she has met with the opponent in private to clarify some elements of each side's proposals.

As negotiations proceed, angry exchanges continue, while negotiators narrow the number of unresolved issues and begin to seriously consider each other's financial proposals. Near the deadline the frequency of moves and countermoves increases; with each move the negotiating teams recede from the main table to meet alone. Meanwhile, on the side, lead bargainers meet more often in private. In the final flurry of activity before the contract expires, the two sides settle on an economic plan, complex or unresolved issues are dropped, and the final agreement is rushed to members, hot off the presses after all-night bargaining.

While not every negotiation occurs exactly like this, this scenario captures the essence and tone of the process. There is, as the International Harvester manager put it, a script to negotiations which is collectively understood and largely followed. The complaints that can be leveled against this process are fairly apparent: It reinforces antagonisms between the two sides, the conversations are highly constrained, and many people are unable to contribute. In a more passionate critique, a newcomer to the labor negotiation process describes the negotiation process as

an intricate, psychological war of wills and nerve between self-interested adversaries. At best, the value of the adversarial system of resolving conflict is vastly overrated. At worst, it can devastate human relationships and an institution. Basically honest people have purposefully distorted their perceptions to such an extent that they have been able to institutionalize dishonesty (Cherim 1982, 14).

To return to our earlier question: Why does this pattern appear in so many negotiations? Why do people act in ways that conform to it and reproduce it? Why is it so stable and persistent?

Theories of Negotiation

Economics and Game Theory

One branch of economic theory and industrial relations does not address the negotiation process at all. These scholars (see Kochan 1980 for a review) are interested in predicting aggregate outcomes, such as average wage increases in a given year or the number of negotiations that result in strikes, but not the results of any particular negotiation. They explain these aggregate outcomes in terms of structural or economic variables, such as unemployment level, the substitutability of labor in the production process, or the existence of pattern bargaining, but do not look at all at the negotiation process itself. From this macro perspective the negotiation process is treated as a black box and ignored.

Microeconomists and game theorists do look inside the black box, but they focus primarily on the outcome not the process. This approach to research is highly stylized and mathematical. Negotiators are assumed to be completely rational: They know exactly what they want, are consistent in their desires, and proceed to make choices in a utility-maximizing fashion. With that starting point, game theorists construct an abstract negotiation game, with defined payoffs for the parties and rules for how the parties must make their decisions.[4] Once the game is construct-

---

4. A common rule, for example (used in Nash's 1950 classic paper on bargaining games), is that negotiators can only settle for agreements where one party cannot get more without hurting the other party (this is called "Pareto optimal" by economists).

ed, and it is assumed that both parties are rational and have all relevant information, each move and countermove can be specified and a final point of agreement can be identified. In this way the game has a determinate solution.

This approach to the study of negotiations has been criticized from several directions. Bacharach and Lawler (1988) point out that the restrictions that game theorists place on decision making are not ones that are realistic, and that no attention is paid to environmental constraints.[5] Moreover predicted results are often a variant of "meet in the middle" or "split the difference," which is not very informative: "What one needs to explain is not why actors will tend to split the difference but when they will choose to observe such a rule and how they will interpret that rule once they have decided to apply it" (pp. 15–16). And Young (1975) points out that game theory eliminates strategic interaction from the analysis even though that is the core phenomenon of bargaining: If strategic choices were allowed, there would be no way to specify every move and countermove, and thus no way to arrive at a determinate solution. Game theory does not model the negotiation process that actually happens but rather the logical steps of idealized rational actors playing out rules that are set by the theorist.

Microeconomic models take a different approach. Influenced largely by observations of labor negotiations, "economists treat bargaining as a process of convergence over time involving a sequence of offers and counteroffers on the part of participants" (Young 1975, 131). The question they address is: With each move, will a negotiator make a concession or hold tight? And, at what point will an equilibrium be reached? The answer is based

---

5. Young (1975) points out that in order to achieve its mathematical elegance and clear solutions, game theory *must* "abstract away a number of problems that many students of decision making regard as highly important in a wide variety of real world situations" (p. 23). Recently some attempts have been made to apply more realistic assumptions to game theory, such as aysmetric information, but these changes usually result in nondeterminate solutions (Canning 1989).

on some form of utility-maximizing analysis. Zeuthen (1930), for example, argues that a negotiator's decision to make a concession is based on a comparison of the expected value of the concession versus the expected value of holding out for the most desired outcome (including the possibility of no agreement). For Hicks (1932) the equilibrium outcome is determined by each side's tolerance for a strike: As the length of a strike is expected to increase, each side will concede more (the cost of the no-agreement alternative has increased) so that a point of agreement is reached.

These models, like game theory, are oversimplified representations of the negotiation process: They include only two negotiators, each of whom is treated as a monolithic entity, and has preferences that are consistent and stable over time (Young 1975). There is no discussion of how preferences are formed, perceptions of costs and benefits are shaped, or how each move is made. The interesting problem is not defining the equilibrium point in the abstract, but how the parties learn enough about each other to find that abstract equilibrium point. Bacharach and Lawler (1988) point out that, like game theorists, economists provide a "definition of the problem that bargainers face without specifying the process by which the parties solve it" (p. 21).

Social Psychology

While economists and game theorists model the behaviors of theoretically constructed rational actors, social psychologists study how real people respond to negotiating situations. Using bargaining simulations and students as subjects, social psychologists have explored the relationship between bargaining outcomes and hundreds of variables (literally!), including personality, negotiating experience, time limits, degree of cooperativeness, language, and the physical layout of the negotiations (Rubin and

Brown 1975; Pruitt 1981; Lewicki and Litterer 1985). In recent years the dominant issue has been the question of negotiator rationality. Contrary to the assumptions of economists and game theorists, Max Bazerman, Magaret Neale, and a generation of students from Northwestern University have documented in great detail the fact that most people are not very rational negotiators: Perceptions are influenced by arbitrary factors such as how an offer is phrased and the size of the initial offer, negotiators tend to search only for information that confirms their judgments, and negotiators tend to ignore the perceptions of the other party (Bazerman and Neale 1992; Neale and Bazerman 1991).

This research provides a treasure trove of insights but, like game theory, is limited by its own strength. The experimental method provides "especially clear-cut evidence about cause and effect" (Pruitt 1981, 10), yet that clarity is achieved at the cost of realism:

The simulated settings employed are likely to differ in many ways from the real-life settings to which one wishes to generalize. For example, the following features of most experiments are unusual in professional negotiation: Negotiators are college students, time is severely compressed, past and future relations between the parties are limited or nonexistent, negotiators are told what issues and options to consider, their values and priorities are specified rather than freely chosen, and negotiation is sponsored by a mysterious authority figure—the experimenter. (p. 12)

In these ways experimental research "decontextualizes" conflict (Barley 1991). It shows us how variables affect others when they are isolated experimentally, but in actual negotiations people have to deal simultaneously with all of the emotional, cognitive, personal, and interpersonal issues identified by social psychologists. In particular, group dynamics are mostly ignored. There are studies on "multiparty" negotiations (e.g., Mannix 1993), but these studies still treat negotiators as single units; the research question in these cases is how coalitions will form among several individuals, not how groups affect the negotiation process.

Prescriptive Theories

Prescriptive theorists take process seriously. They show that the outcome of negotiations is not just a matter of two parties arriving mysteriously at the analyst's equilibrium point; it is affected by how negotiators interpret the situation, shape perceptions, and create or eliminate options. The reality that negotiators work with is socially constructed (Berger and Luckman 1967). From a competitive perspective, negotiators can gain more by hiding from the opponent what they would really accept and convincing the opponent that their position cannot be changed. They can also gain by tying their own hands. If one side can commit itself to a position, the opponent then faces the option of accepting that position or failing to have any agreement at all (Schelling 1960). Commitments are made by making public promises to constituents, by imposing penalties on oneself so that backing down is too costly, or by cutting off communication. It can also help to appear irrational, so that even if the opponent knows that it makes sense to back down (in terms of costs and benefits), they cannot be sure that you will do so. To gain competitive advantage, one wants to communicate as little as possible, communicate inaccurate information, bluff, and act irrationally.

From an integrative perspective (Mary Parker Follett 1942; Pruitt 1981; Susskind and Cruikshank 1987), negotiators can gain more by first making sure that they produce as much value as possible. In economic terms this means moving the parties toward the Pareto frontier or pushing that frontier farther out. To get there, negotiators need to be clear-headed, unemotional, and creative. More specifically, they need to "focus on interests not positions, separate the people from the problem, invent options for mutual gain, and insist on objective criteria" (Fisher and Ury 1981).

These prescriptive theories explain some basic negotiation strategies but do not tell us how and why those strategies have been transformed into the particular routines that we see in labor negotiations. Competitive bargaining theory explains why labor negotiators would want to hide information but does not explain the way they do that hiding, or why they sometimes convey information through signaling and sidebar discussions. Integrative bargaining theory explains why labor negotiators might want to convey information but does not explain the way they convey information in labor negotiations, or why they spend so much time grandstanding, building acrimony, and hiding information. What is missing from these theories, again, is social context. The perceptions that negotiators in labor relations have to shape are not just those of the opponent but also those of constituents and teammates. Moreover, while managing these perceptions is clearly important for strategic reasons, it may be important for other—more personal and interpersonal—reasons as well.

Institutional Theories

In contrast to the abstracted models of negotiation just described, the institutional literature on negotiation provides rich, thick descriptions of the process. Some of the better known studies of this type for labor negotiations include those done by Douglas (1962), Peters (1955), and Selekman (1947). The seminal work in this line of research is Walton and McKersie's *A Behavioral Theory of Labor Negotiations*. They synthesized the previous research, as well as their own, and created a general theory of negotiations. Their model has four subprocesses. First, "distributive" bargaining occurs when each side tries to get more for itself. Second, "integrative" bargaining occurs when the two sides try to make both sides better off. Third, "attitudinal restructuring" occurs when negotiators try to shape the attitudes of the other party toward themselves. Fourth, "intraorganizational bargaining" occurs when negotiators negotiate with their own constituents. Walton and McKersie show that integrative and distributive bargaining occur together in labor negotiations, and they identify the existence of attitudinal restructuring and intraorganizational bargaining. Their book has become a classic in the negotiation literature and one of the most widely cited books on labor relations.

What Walton and McKersie leave underdeveloped is an understanding of how negotiators manage to deal with all four subprocesses at once. Do negotiators do both integrative and distributive bargaining at the same time? Do the same people do both? How do they avoid falling to cross-purposes, given the different behavioral requirements of each?[6] Also, how do attitudinal restructuring and intraorganizational bargaining relate to each other and to the first two elements of bargaining?[7]

A Dramaturgical Approach

To focus on the social dimensions of negotiations and understand their impact on the negotiation process, I will analyze them from a dramaturgical perspective. The notion that social interaction is in many ways similar to drama was introduced by Erving Goffman (1959). When people interact with others, they can be thought of as actors, taking on established social roles

---

6. Lax and Sebenius (1986) highlight the tension between integrative and distributive tactics and refer to it as the "negotiator's dilemma."

7. Tracy and Peterson (1986) argue that little research has been done on Walton and McKersie's (1965) full model because the four subprocesses were never integrated. In a twenty-five year retrospective on Walton and McKersie's book at the Academy of Management meetings (1990), Roy Lewicki observed that researchers have paid a great deal of attention to the distinction between integrative and distributive bargaining, but they have tended to see this distinction in either-or terms (which was not what Walton and McKersie intended) and have mostly ignored attitudinal restructuring and intraorganizational bargaining.

such as a teacher or student or enemy or friend. These roles then have associated with them particular behaviors, or, as Goffman puts it, "fronts." A front includes "posture, speech patterns, facial expressions, bodily gestures" (p. 24); it includes both how actors appear and how they behave. The front conveys an idealized version of the actor; for example, if one takes on the role of teacher, the goal is to appear like a flawless teacher, who is energetic, skilled, and fully identified with that role. A performance may also convey an idealized version of the community:

> To the degree that a performance highlights the common official values of the society in which it occurs, we may look upon it, in the manner of Durkheim and Radcliffe-Brown, as a ceremony—as an expressive rejuvenation and reaffirmation of the moral values of the community. (p. 35)

When people take on a role, some effort is needed for the performance to be accepted.[8] First, the performance must be appropriate: It must be "molded and modified to fit into the understanding and expectations of the society in which it is presented" (p. 35). Second, the performance must be well executed. This requires that actors "forgo or conceal action that is inconsistent with" the ideal that is being conveyed. Third it requires a great deal of expressive control. As Goffman puts it, "even sympathetic audiences can be momentarily disturbed, shocked, and weakened in their faith by the discovery of a picayune discrepancy in the impressions presented to them . . . a single note off key can disrupt the tone of an entire presentation" (pp. 51–52). In sum, actors must take pains to fulfill the role they are playing:

> A status, a position, a social place is not a material thing, to be possessed and then displayed; it is a pattern of appropriate conduct, coherent, embellished, and well articulated. Performed with ease or clumsiness, awareness

---

8. Socialization into a new profession, for example, requires that individuals learn how to conduct themselves in a fashion that convinces others (and themselves) that they are who they claim to be. For medical students there is a long process of learning and internalizing the appropriate attitude of a doctor, such as "detatched concern" (Lief and Fox 1963).

or not, guile or good faith, it is nonetheless something that must be enacted and portrayed, something that must be realized. (p. 75)

This is not meant to imply that behaviors are scripted in any comprehensive way, or that actors learn specific detailed actions for each part. There "could not be enough time or energy for this," as Goffman puts it. Rather, "what does seem to be required of the individual is that he learn enough pieces of expression to be able to 'fill in' and manage, more or less, any part that he is likely to be given" (Goffman, p. 73).

Note that actors both influence and are influenced by the audience. The audience brings expectations to the performance, observes the actors, and responds to their performance.[9] If the performance is deemed appropriate and well executed, the response is positive. If the performance is deemed inappropriate or is poorly performed, the response is negative.[10] At the same time actors shape the impressions of the audience. They try to convince the audience that they are who they claim to be, to motivate them in turn to behave in ways that are desired by the actor and to get the audience to see the world in the way that they have defined it.[11]

---

9. This approach is consistent with role theory. Traditional role theory points out that social behaviors are patterned and explains these patterns by looking at the "bundles of socially defined attributes and expectations associated with social positions" (Abercrombie, Hill, and Turner 1984, 180). Expectations are publicly understood, learned through experience, and reinforced by observers. This process is called "role sending" by Kahn, Wolfe, Quinn, Snoek, and Rosenthal (1964).

10. Violations of expected behaviors may cause anger or shock in others, leading to sanctions against the actor or withdrawal from the interaction by other actors. In experiments conducted by Garfinkel (1967) subjects were very disturbed when Garfinkel's students acted in ways that were not "normal" (e.g., acting like a stranger toward one's spouse). In some cases people simply refuse to acknowledge nonnormal behaviors; as Sudnow (1965) documented, public defenders do not look at crimes in terms of what happened but rather in terms of what type of "normal" crime comes closest to what the person did.

11. There is a rich tradition of research dedicated to understanding ways in which people try to shape the perceptions of others. Schlenker (1980) reviews various elements of "impression management," including excuses, giving accounts, justifying actions, and deception. Hochschild (1983) describes the ways in which airline stew-

On a broader level actors are both influenced by and influence the social structure.[12] Social structure determines the array of social positions that are filled by actors; the division of labor and management into two sides, for example, creates the social role of opponent. And the behaviors associated with a role are publicly understood prior to the move by any individual into that role. As Goffman put it, "when an actor takes on an established social role, usually he finds that a particular front has already been established for it" (p. 27). At the same time the social structure is reproduced only when the actors play the defined roles. Actors are constantly negotiating over the social order (Strauss 1978) and their place in it. Much of what actors are trying to convey is a definition of how people are organized into groups, who is in what group, and how those groups relate to each other. In this sense, as Goffman indicated above, patterned social behavior is more than just a routine—it is ceremony (or "ritual," to use a word that is more common today) when the purpose is to collectively reaffirm the definition of how society is organized.[13]

The elements of the model described so far include the actor, the audience, and the performance. The actor is the person who is playing a role in the presence of others with the intent of having an impact on them. The audience is those who observe the

---

ardesses try to convince customers of the emotions they are feeling. On a broader level, Gusfield has looked at ways in which groups shape reality to meet their interests (1963, 1981), and Edelman (1977) examines the rhetoric of politics.

12. Symbolic interactionists, such as Mead (1934) and Turner (1975) see roles emerging from interaction with others. Since then, sociologists have tended to stake out more extreme positions, believing either in human choice or in the force of social structure. More recently social theorists have tried to articulate a view of social action that does not eliminate either choice or social structure. Bourdieu (1977), for example, has argued that people do make choices, but their understanding of what outcomes will result from their choices is based on their observations of past results of similar actions, which is influenced by social structure.

13. Rituals, according to Leach (1968), are actions that serve to express the status of the actor and those in the community: "Our day-to-day relationships depend upon a mutual knowledge and mutual acceptance of the fact that at any particular time any two individuals occupy different positions in a highly complex network of status relationships; ritual serves to reaffirm what these status differences are" (p. 524).

actor. It includes anyone whom the actor knows is watching, and whose responses, judgments, and acceptance of their performance affect the actor. The performance is a series of actions carried out by the actor in order to conform to role expectations and influence the audience. A performance may be simply a routine—a pattern of activity that is repeated simply because that is how it is done—or it may have collective meaning and thus serve the function of a ceremony or ritual. Throughout this book, we will see, the negotiation process is more ritual than routine.

The last element of the model that must be introduced is the notion of stage. Front stage, actors are visible to the audience and have to stay in role. Backstage, actors can relax from their roles, step out of character, and work with their dramaturgical teammates to prepare for the front stage performance. For actors, their ability to manage their exposure to role expectations depends on their ability to move on and off the front stage. In negotiations, we will see, this is particularly important; contradictory role expectations are obviated largely through a process of moving, physically or conceptually, between front and back stages. This distinction also helps us see how the different elements of Walton and McKersie's model are managed. Distributive bargaining occurs largely on the front stage of maintable negotiations; integrative bargaining occurs largely backstage in private meetings between lead bargainers or in caucus meetings on each side. Intraorganizational bargaining occurs largely in the backstage of caucus meetings, and attitudinal restructuring occurs largely in the backstage of sidebar meetings. The ability of negotiators to engage in all elements of Walton and McKersie's model depends on their ability to construct backstage environments as well as the front stage drama, and to manage the movement between these stages.

A dramaturgical theory of negotiations is a theory about the negotiation process. It focuses on all behaviors in negotiations, not just how bids are made and when concessions are given. Negotiator actions are certainly influenced by strategic logic of the type presented by Schelling (1960) or Fisher and Ury (1981), but they are also influenced by role expectations and the desire to perform one's role well,[14] create perceptions in the audience, and remind everyone of how society is organized. The issue is not to determine whether negotiators are rational or not but to understand the many different concerns, pressures, and goals that motivate their behavior. Most of the time negotiators are quite sensible (or rational, if you will); it is just that they are being sensible about many things that are not visible in a payoff matrix or utility curve.

The negotiation process therefore is not an arbitrary set of actions. It is a carefully crafted ritual that has evolved to achieve a set of practical and symbolic goals. The barrier to change lies not in negotiator irrationality but in the fact that the traditional process represents the way in which sensible people respond to the role structure of labor negotiations. The current system, we will see, enables negotiators to manage constituent pressures, maintain group identity, and act as leaders of a team.

Research Process

My study of negotiations took a long and circuitous path. I began by studying one historical case in great depth; my study of International Harvester's six-month-long strike in 1979 included over 100 interviews with negotiators, labor leaders, managers, and workers. I visited four of the cities where IH had plants, meeting with people in lunchrooms, bars, union offices,

---

14. Kolb (1983) makes a similar argument about the behavior of mediators in labor negotiations. She argues that mediators do not analyze the case, decide on a strategy, and then determine what role they should play. Rather, it is their preestablished and institutionally defined role that shapes what strategy they believe is sensible, which in turn shapes how they analyze the case. Mediator behavior is driven by roles, not strategy.

and corporate offices. I learned from that study, among other things, that negotiators had very strong expectations about the negotiation process, and that they counted on the fact that others would use the established process (Friedman 1989). The attempt to change that process on the part of IH management—to unilaterally impose a kind of naive rationality on the ritual of negotiations—proved fatal to the negotiations and the relationship between labor and management.

After that study was complete, I yearned for a more "scientific" comparison of negotiations that would "prove" that the negotiation process makes a difference. I set out to find cases that were alike in all respects but the process so that differences in outcome could be attributed to this difference. I was lucky enough to identify one case of this type, and interviewed many of the participants at two bargaining tables within New Bell Publishing Corporation (Friedman and Gal 1991). I soon realized, however, that my attempt to be so careful was problematic: Finding a controlled comparison in labor negotiations was like finding a needle in a haystack and limited my study to historical cases. After hearing so much about the process, I needed to be there myself. I wanted to know how it felt to be in negotiations, what the tone of the conversations were, and what kinds of things were actually said and by whom. I could learn a great deal from interviews, but I would understand the process in different ways if I had direct access to them.

As a result I tried to gain access to negotiations that were in process. This proved to be quite difficult. Given the secrecy of negotiations, what is at stake, and the degree to which players feel the spotlight on them, most negotiators do not want outside observers. After many months passed with no leads, I realized that I needed to be more proactive in my search; it would take many requests for access before I received a single positive response, and I was beginning to wonder if I would be fortunate enough to get access to any negotiations at all. In the meantime I interviewed nineteen union leaders, labor relations managers, and labor lawyers who were known to be experienced negotiators. If I could not learn about negotiations in greater depth by attending them, at least I could broaden my range of knowledge by interviewing as many negotiators as possible. At the same time I met with students at Harvard's Trade Union Program to get feedback about my ideas. Of course I left every interview and meeting saying: If you are going to negotiate a contract and think I might be able to observe, please give me a call. To my great surprise, I gained access to six negotiations in this way (Hartford Centrum, House-Chem Industries, Lowell Animal Shelter, Brick Industries, Connecticut Hospital, and Eastern Pigment).

In each of these cases I entered negotiations from one side or the other. At House-Chem Industries and Lowell Animal Shelter, my access was from the management side. For the others, it was from the union side. In two of the union cases the union negotiators took me with them to negotiations with the belief that it was their prerogative to have someone attend negotiations on their side. In these cases I was tolerated by management for the day or two that I was already in town, but thereafter was informed that my visits were over. In all of the cases I promised all parties that I would not reveal anything about the individuals or institutions involved, and would do nothing to interfere with the process. As I sat watching the negotiations or caucus meetings, I took notes about what was said and my impressions about the attitudes of the different parties and the tone of the meetings.[15] I tried to talk with negotiators between meetings, and had more

---

15. In some cases I could not attend all of the negotiations due to scheduling difficulties. In anticipation of that problem, a research assistant, Caitlin Deinard, accompanied me and took notes during my absence. She was well accepted by the negotiators, knew what was happening, and learned to observe and record both the content and process of negotiations. At Midwestern University, another research assistant, Shahaf Gal, took notes and recorded meetings during a week that I could not attend.

elaborate and focused discussions with the lead bargainer after the meetings for the day were over. The interviews were as important as the observations since they gave me access to the negotiators' thoughts and allowed me to see how different people were experiencing the same situation.

At the same time I had the good fortune to be invited to join a research team studying the application of "mutual gains bargaining" to labor negotiations. Mutual gains bargaining is the approach to negotiation that has been popularized in recent years by Fisher and Ury (1981). It proposes that negotiators talk about interests, not positions, in the hope that this will help each side to solve the others' problems in ways that cost them as little as possible. Toward that end negotiators set aside a time to invent as many options as possible, they avoid letting the conflict become personal, and they look for objective criteria to evaluate the options. This process is taught through lectures, games, and elaborate simulations where the negotiators try to model the new process prior to actual bargaining. The Program on Negotiation received a grant from the Department of Labor to bring the training to three sites.

For each of these cases my entry was as a member of a research team during the training. As a researcher, rather than a trainer, I conducted surveys,[16] interviewed people, and observed negotiators during the training sessions and discussions. I watched what was happening with a skeptical eye, not wanting to prejudge the new process as either a success or failure. In two of the cases I was allowed access to negotiations following the training. In one of these cases (Western Technologies) I attended negotiations and a few union caucuses. In the other case (Midwestern University) I attended negotiations and caucus meetings on both sides and tape-recorded all meetings. In both

---

16. Some results from the quantitative aspect of this research is reported in Friedman and Podolny (1992) and Friedman (1993a).

cases there were some negotiators who saw me initially as a facilitator for the new process; after the first few days it was clear that I was a neutral observer.

The final case came as a result of my previous study at New Bell Publishing. Having heard of my involvement with mutual gains bargaining, I was brought in by the company and union as a consultant (together with a colleague) to provide training in mutual gains bargaining for their next round of negotiations. This was my first time to play the role of advocate for MGB. In the end they did not use the process and I did not attend the negotiations, but I interviewed the company's lead bargainer repeatedly about the negotiations.

All together I studied thirteen negotiations, with varying degrees of access and intensity (see table 1.1). These negotiations also varied in size, from small bargaining units of 30–100 employees (the last six cases of table 1.1), to larger units with

Table 1.1
List of cases

Name of case	Data collected
International Harvester	Post-hoc interviews (100)
New Bell Publishing, 1986 (Nebraska)	Post-hoc interviews (30)
New Bell Publishing, 1986 (Minnesota)	Post-hoc interviews (30)
New Bell Publishing, 1990	Training, debriefing, interviews
Texas Bell	Training, interviews, surveys
Western Technologies	Training, observation (2 months), interviews, surveys
Midwestern University	Training, observation (3 months), interviews, surveys
Hartford Centrum	Observation (6 days over 2 months)
House-Chem Industries	Observation (6 days over 2 months)
Lowell Animal Shelter	Observation (8 days over 1 month)
Brick Industries	Partial observation (1 day)
Connecticut Hospital	Partial observation (2 days)
Eastern Pigment	Partial observation (2 days)

500–1000 employees (Midwestern, Western Technologies), to multiple-site negotiations with hundreds (New Bell) or thousands (International Harvester, Texas Bell) of employees.

From all of these cases I learned about the traditional labor negotiation process. In most of the cases the negotiations were quite routine and normal. Although there were great differences among these cases, as would be true of any sample of negotiations, they were ones where nothing was being done to change the traditional process in any way. In other cases there were efforts by some of the parties to change the process. These cases provided information not only about the change process itself but also about the traditional process. That is because change often makes people defend old ways, feel their importance, and articulate the logic of those patterns in a way that may not be possible in normal times.[17] In normal times behaviors may be driven by "background expectations" that are not visible to the actors themselves, and, even where actors are aware of the process, there is no reason to explain them to others.

Throughout this process, my theoretical perspective was continually evolving. I began the study with a concern for the underlying cultural elements of negotiations (influenced largely by the work of Schutz 1962, Garfinkel 1967, and Bourdieu 1977) and a conviction that negotiators, like all people, are situated in a network of social relations (Granovetter 1985) that influences their actions. As I learned about the rituals of bargaining, I tried to uncover the assumptions and motivations of the people who enacted these rituals, and why the rituals seemed to be so impor-

---

17. One branch of sociology (Garfinkel 1967) has developed a research methodology based explicitly on this phenomenon. In this approach researchers consciously breach expected routines, then watch the reactions. It is only through such a process that background assumptions that govern everyday life are revealed—it is only by seeing the kinds of anger, confusion, or disruption caused by breaches of the routine that we can come to understand the functions that routines play in people's lives.

tant to them. The more I observed negotiators in action, the more I sensed negotiators' concern that they feel and appear competent in their roles as negotiators, and realized that this problem presented quite a challenge. I also noticed that negotiators were greatly concerned with impressions, and changed their behavior depending on who was watching. As I began to write about my observations, colleagues commented that I was describing the process more and more in terms of a drama—speaking of roles, audiences, and performances. The language of dramaturgy seemed to capture much of what goes on in labor negotiations, incorporate my earlier theoretical perspective, and provide a way to organize my observations.

In the end the reader is left with my reporting of the data and my interpretation of it. That is influenced by the theoretical perspective I brought with me to the study, how I collected the data, and the way in which the story is told. I hope that the interpretation is well documented and convincing, but it is still my interpretation.[18] My goal is to create a model of the negotiation process that retains enough of its complexity to go beyond the issues typically covered in the study of negotiations, but also one that is focused enough to direct our attention to particular aspects of the process that need to be recognized. The model should be judged on whether it rings true to observers and practitioners, and provides a clear way of understanding an important and overlooked aspect of the negotiation process.

---

18. This is true, I believe, of all social science. Even when statistics are used, there is as much interpretation and "construction of reality" as there is in qualitative research, but without the seemingly scientific veneer of numbers, the subjective aspect of qualitative research is made more apparent. Van Maanen (1988) argues that ethnographies inevitably involve the skilled telling of tales, the authority for which is based mostly on the credibility of the writer and his or her observations. In his scheme, my analysis involves "realist" tales.

The Plan of the Book

Part I of this book is about the traditional process of negotiations. A dramaturgical model of that process is developed, piece
by piece, starting with negotiators' roles as opponents (chapter
2), representatives (chapter 3), and leaders (chapter 4). With the
role structure defined, the process is examined in terms of what
happens on both the front and back stages of negotiations (chapter 5), and the logic and limits of this system are examined
(chapter 6). Throughout this analysis, no cases are presented in
full; rather, pieces of cases are used to highlight relevant elements of the negotiation process and build a picture of an "ideal
type" negotiation (Weber 1947). The model is intended to capture the essence of the negotiation process; no single case is likely to be played out exactly as described in this ideal model.

Having explained the logic behind the traditional ritual in
part I, several negotiations are examined in part II where the traditional ritual was changed. In one case negotiators worked
around those rituals (chapter 7), in another they ignored them
(chapter 8), and in another they redefined the rituals (chapter 9).
The last of these three is a case of mutual gains bargaining. Since
that approach is drawing a great deal of attention currently,
additional attempts to bring mutual gains bargaining to labor
relations are described in the following chapter (chapter 10). The
final chapter discusses the logic and limits of changing the traditional way in which labor and management negotiate.

I

The Social Logic of
the Negotiation Ritual

2   Defining Groups: Whose Side Are You On?

One of the most obvious and seemingly trivial observations that can be made about labor negotiations is the fact that there are two sides: labor and management (figure 2.1)[1]. I suggest that this basic "fact" is not so obvious and certainly not trivial. The division of people into labor and management is not the only way that subgroups could have formed; it is a legal definition of the situation that has to be enacted, reinforced, and performed in order to be made socially real. Norms of behavior and sanctions against inappropriate actions are what make this definition of the situation into reality. At the same time the division of people into two distinct groups—legally and socially—has implications for the way they communicate, whether information is understood, and the kinds of behavior that are deemed acceptable among members. This chapter is about the basic division of negotiators into two sides: why it exists, how it is maintained, and the implications of its existence.

Isn't the Division Natural?

The division of labor and management is central to the rhetoric of labor-management relations and shapes the thinking of many

---

1. As additional dimensions of the social structure of bargaining are examined in chapters 3 and 4, additional elements will be added to figure 2.1.

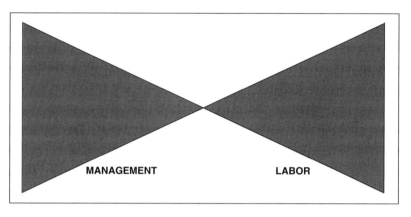

Figure 2.1
Labor versus management

union leaders and managers, but it is certainly not true that this happened naturally. Historically laborers in the skilled trades identified themselves as apprentices to masters, who were independent businessmen of high status (Dore 1973, 54). With the growth of large companies with centralized and distant management structures, those in the skilled trades saw themselves in terms of craft groups; in their eyes they were as distinct from the laboring masses as they were from managers. The very notion of combining the skilled trade unions of the AFL with unskilled common laborers of the CIO was anathema to their sense of status and identity (Mills 1989). Even today those in the "skilled trades" within large plants see themselves as a separate elite.

There are natural differences and divisions among groups in the United States, but these do not line up consistently with their relation to the "means of production," as Marxists would put it.[2]

---

2. Noting the American union movement's lack of socialist political tendencies, Bok and Dunlop (1970) report that "the opinions of union members are particularly striking in their lack of any special class bias" (p. 46). They explain this finding in terms of American history—the great heterogeneity among immigrant workers, the opportunity to move west and own land, and the fast growth of American industry and thus of wages for skilled workers.

Race and ethnicity, rather than occupation or class, drive local politics (Katznelson 1981) and provide one of the most salient social divisions at work. At an engine plant I visited in Indianapolis, African-American workers predominated in the hot, dirty, dangerous foundry part of the plant, while whites predominated in the relatively clean and safe assembly part of the plant. One white worker commented about black workers in the foundry, "They like it over there." At many companies African-American managers have formed network groups to support each other and overcome racial barriers (Friedman and Deinard 1991; Friedman and Carter 1993). Similar groups exist for Hispanics, Asians, and women.

If we look at the legal definition of management and workers, we find great potential for ambiguity. Are lower-level managers employees or employers? At one time, foremen could be in unions, but current legal definitions of the labor-management distinction keep them out of unions (Kochan 1980, 136). There has been much wrangling in colleges and universities over the status of faculty. Based on the Yeshiva decision, faculty in private schools are currently deemed to be managers and therefore unable to organize, while faculty in state schools can and do organize. Apparently many people feel, regardless of legal definitions, that they are the subjects of management rather than the providers of it.

Unions themselves are often seen to dominate workers as much as managers do. In some cases union leaders have become an elite class of their own, with special privileges and extreme power. The Landrum-Griffin Act was created to ensure that worker representation by unions is actually and equitably provided to all bargaining unit members and that democratic processes are used in the election of union officials (Bok and Dunlop 1970). One indicator of the ambiguity inherent in the division between labor and management is the fact that satisfaction with the union is *positively* related to satisfaction with the company (see, e.g., Purcell 1954).

The effects of cross-cutting ties can be seen at the bargaining table as well. Among the cases observed for this book, the creation of a unified team was often difficult. At Texas Bell there was, at times, as much antagonism between rural and urban segments of the union as between labor and management; at New Bell Publishing, between clerical workers and salespeople. On the management side, labor relations managers at IH were frustrated with line managers who did not follow the rules, while line managers saw the labor relations staff as bureaucrats;[3] managers on the Texas Bell bargaining team at times worried more about how they could manage their boss than how to negotiate with the union. For both management and the union, negotiations were often led by people sent from corporate headquarters, a law firm, or the International union who were all more like each other than like the people on their "side."

Why does the simple distinction between labor and management usually dominate negotiations? On one level the distinction is legally mandated. Once a bargaining unit is certified by the National Labor Relations Board, representatives of that bargaining unit and management are required to sit down and negotiate the wages and working conditions of the represented employees. But this legal definition does not necessarily make the distinction socially real, nor does it require antagonism, dislike, or a rigid separation between the parties. There are differences between the two parties, for sure, but as we saw above, the common interests of workers or managers represent only one dimension of cleavage that might be salient. What makes these differences so palpable and real?

---

3. Dunlop (1984) argues that labor relations experts from different organizations have a greater community of interest with each other than with others in their hierarchy.

Public Rhetoric: Highlighting Differences

Prior to negotiations unions often highlight the differences
between workers and managers in public presentations. In
speeches, during rallies, and in publications they emphasize not
only what they have in common as workers but also the ways in
which management stands apart as their common enemy. In
UAW publications such as *Solidarity* and *AMMO*, for example,
attention is drawn to management's callousness, including
widespread safety violations, union-busting campaigns, and
"bloated" executive salaries. Mixed in with current concerns are
constant reminders of the past, such as when Walter Reuther
was beaten by Ford "service department" thugs in the 1930s and
Michigan National Guard troops aimed machine guns at workers. These stories remind workers of their common interests, the
potential threat that management poses, and the need to have a
union to protect workers from abuses. As Schudson (1986)
argues, the "mobilization of memory is an important instrument
of social action." At Texas Bell the union's publication for members depicted management as a mean drug dealer offering workers a needle filled with "givebacks" (see figure 2.2). In the same
publication a commentary pointed out that "too many of the
current crop of American corporate executives think that vast
personal wealth is the singular purpose of a corporation. Once
they bleed a corporation of its assets, they feel no compunction
about casting its people aside and proceeding to the scene of
their next crime." And, when the maverick Hotel Workers'
union in Boston sought to gain housing benefits, it united its
diverse members by showing them pictures of the hotel owners'
luxurious homes.

Public rhetoric of this type is not so common among managers. As is discussed below, management does not need to
mobilize its membership the same way that the union does.

Figure 2.2
UTW's depiction of management (printed by permission of Mike Konopacki, Huck/Konopacki Labor Cartoons)

And, after negotiations, management needs to convince workers that they are a respected part of the corporate "team"—public pronouncements that the union and the workers they represent are the enemy would be counterproductive. Moreover management is not given to emotional displays. For managers to show their anger, argues Jackall (1988), "is seen as irrational, unbefitting men or women whose principal claim to social legitimacy is dispassionate rational calculation" (p. 49). Managers, he says, "need to exercise iron self-control and to have the ability to mask all emotion and intention behind bland, smiling, and agreeable public faces. . . . Sometimes this may mean suppressing the natural desire to defend oneself" (pp. 47–48).

During negotiations the differences between the two sides are reinforced by both sides in a less public way. Teammates are taught to maintain a united front—showing group unity and serving as dramaturgical teammates for each other. And, during caucuses they devote time to reminding each other of the negative qualities of the other side.

Bargaining Rituals: Acting as a Team

The effort to show a united front is consciously maintained during negotiations. At the Connecticut Hospital negotiations, for example, the union's lead bargainer explicitly coached her team on how to behave. She asked them to rehearse their arguments, then assigned those arguments to particular people: "You do the 'sacrifice of the past' argument, you do the 'insurance is your responsibility' argument, and I will do the 'flagship' argument. Otherwise, we will caucus. Stay poker faced. Except, if *we* talk, all nod your head." These negotiators were taught not to disagree in public: If there were any problems or disagreements, they would caucus and discuss those issues in private. At the same time they were taught that they were teammates in a carefully crafted performance.

When negotiations actually begin, the sense of unity is maintained by sitting together opposite the opponents and by physically breaking into separate private caucus meetings whenever complex issues need to be discussed or the performance is at risk. These actions show each side that it is a separate group, with secret agendas and a distinct group identity. Each group knows that there is a backstage where the other side prepares and practices its performance and that it is allowed by the other side to see only a carefully crafted image.

These displays of unity have obvious strategic benefits (they enable negotiators to control the flow of information), but they also help remind teammates that they are a group. For the purposes of negotiations, internal differences are suspended: In public the only acknowledged distinction is between "us" and "them." The audience for this performance is not only the opponent, but also one's own group. It is important both to show the opponent a united front and to create that unity within the team.

Backstage "Conversations of Difference"

Negotiators also learn to highlight the negative aspects of their opponents. In all the cases I observed, I was struck by the degree to which negotiators, when meeting with teammates, would rail against the other side and talk in categorical terms such as "we" and "them," despite the more complex and fine-tuned feelings about the situation that they expressed to me in private. When negotiators met as a team, they usually devoted some time to the negative qualities of the opposing team, and there seemed to be an implicit rule that during this time everyone would agree with each complaint made about the opponent.[4] Despite their differ-

---

4. Geddes (1991) has studied caucus conversations and found that about a third of the conversations are oriented toward analysis of the opponent. These conversations include frequent criticism of the opponent, including humorous "jabs" at them. She found that the lead bargainer tended to come to the defense of the opponent more often.

ences team members did have their opposition to the other side in common.

At Texas Bell union negotiators complained over drinks that management "treated us like dummies" and cared only about keeping workers under their control. Each comment engendered nods of approval around the table. Although most of these negotiators did respect individual managers and most were very concerned about the viability of the company, they held those views in check. There were some bitter intraunion rivalries among these negotiators, but for the moment these were put aside and the focus of attention was on their shared opposition to management. On the management side I heard similar conversations: The union was "incompetent." "They" would never change. In private, both sides talked in terms of "us" versus "them."[5]

The underlying rules for these "conversations of difference," as I call them, appeared to be: (1) Point out ways in which the other side is immoral, unskilled, or in other ways inherently bad, (2) express these feelings in a way that displays anger, frustration, or exasperation with the other side, (3) show how the team, as a group, is better, and (4) show support for each of these sentiments or say nothing at all. Although these meetings were off the front stage of negotiations, teammates had to perform for each other.

Forces of Group Differentiation

Before bargaining begins, during main-table meetings and during caucuses, negotiators enact the difference between labor and

---

5. There is a tendency, when observing "others," to use more adjectives about them than is done when observing those who are in your group (Semin and Fiedler 1989). This use of abstract predicates has a tendency to objectify others, endowing them with seemingly inherent characteristics. Once people begin using abstractions about others, these abstractions become reified as the essence of those others (Fiedler, Semin, and Bolten 1989).

management. Negotiations are governed by implicit rules of behavior that say there should be no public displays of internal disagreements and strong displays of solidarity. These rules guide emotions as well as statements—they include feeling rules[6] that direct people to exhibit and produce emotions that are appropriate to the situation.

In each of these ways negotiators highlight what they have in common with those on their side, the fact that they belong to a group of teammates, the need for that team to show solidarity, and the ways in which the other group is different, nasty, or immoral. They take the legal distinction between the two sides and make it into a difference that is felt emotionally and dominates the actions and thoughts of all parties involved. They make sure that this dimension of everyone's identity is stressed so that the groups "labor" and "management" are made politically and interpersonally real. Why do negotiators do this? The enactment of the labor-management divide is a function of three related phenomena: the importance of difference as a means of mobilizing people (especially for the union), the importance of group distinctions for enhancing group identity, and the tendency of people to conform to group norms as a means of gaining acceptance.

Union Mobilization: Difference as the Basis of Power and Control

Unions, compared to management, are in the unfortunate position of having little formal leverage over their members. The

---

6. An extensive body of literature has developed that identifies the ways in which people are taught to feel and display emotions that are appropriate to the situation. See Hochschild (1975), Schott (1979), Van Maanen and Kunda (1989), and Sutton (1991). At a broader level Douglas (1986) has argued that institutions, such as unions and businesses, channel perceptions so that "they rouse our emotions to a standardized pitch on standardized issues" (p. 92).

union's primary base of power in negotiations is its ability to credibly threaten a strike, and its ability to conduct a strike depends on the willingness of members to cooperate.[7] The union can give orders to its full-time national staff but not to local officers (who answer to the members who elect them) and not to members (technically, members can be fined if they cross a picket line, but they would probably just quit the union as a result). To make matters worse, the benefits provided by the union are a public good (Olson 1965)—individuals receive them whether they contribute or not. If the union negotiates an improved contract, that contract covers everyone in the bargaining unit, not just those who supported the union.[8] And there are no special rewards for those who do cooperate; a few can be offered jobs on the union staff, but not many. "In this respect," according to Flanders (1972), unions

differ, for instance, from business organizations. The latter can grow and expand if they have sufficient money to buy command over the material and human resources they need. People will join them, that is to say, enter their employment, for the sake of the remuneration offered. Trade unions cannot be run simply as businesses. (pp. 22–23)

With no means for providing individual rewards or punishments for members, how can unions create the cooperation that is essential to their mission?

---

7. As the UAW put it in the training brochure, *An Informed Public: How UAW Leaders Can Improve Communication With Union Members and the Community* (1986): "The only real bargaining power the UAW has, ultimately, is the unity and confidence of the membership" (p. 1).

8. The same holds true for other services. If there is a grievance, the union has to represent the person whether he or she is a union member or not. If the union fails to provide full, equal, and unbiased representation to all employees in the bargaining unit, it can be sued for lack of representation. Because of these "free-rider" problems unions usually try to get a clause in their contract that makes the bargaining unit a "union" shop (requiring employees to join the union and pay dues after 30 days on the job), or at least an "agency" shop (requiring those who do not join the union to pay a fee to the union for its services as a bargaining agent). This solves the problem of people benefiting without paying, but not the problem of people benefiting without otherwise supporting the union.

The only way is through the "activation of commitments."[9] To a certain degree the commitments may already be there. But, as we also saw above, workers have many different, overlapping group memberships. There is no reason for them to necessarily see the world in terms of their belonging to the group "labor." Workers have some common interests, but those are not always central; at best they stand as *latent* interests and commonalities. For this set of people to act together, those interests and commonalities have to be highlighted and made active.[10] During times of overt conflict, the creation of a worker consciousness and solidarity occurs naturally (Fantasia 1988). The problem is to engender a common orientation prior to the point of overt conflict.

The public displays of difference mentioned above serve this purpose. They show that the distinction between labor and management is decisive. This distinction defines the group itself—who "we" are—justifies the very existence of the union and provides a reason for members to act in its support. It thereby enables the union to control and coordinate members, and gain power when facing management in negotiations.[11]

Difference as a Basis of Group Identity

In experiments on intergroup relations (Brown 1986), subjects who were placed in groups—based on random assignments and

---

9. Parsons (1963) distinguishes between "situational" means of control—namely factors external to the person, such as wages or punishments, that change their situation—and internal means of control, such as the activation of commitments.

10. Snow Rochford, Worden, and Benford (1986) argue that "collective actors" are created and mobilized by aligning each individual's "framing of a situation," in terms of values, beliefs, and a sense of injustice. Laumann and Marsden (1979) point out that collective actors are created only when communication is established among those who have common interests. In their model, like mine, there is the potential for multiple collective actors, since there are many different issues around which collective actors could form. No one issue separates people cleanly into a single, simple organization of collective actors.

11. This is true especially in large unions that have to organize dispersed members and when unions worry that they will not be taken seriously at the bargaining table.

with no real meaning (e.g., the "blues" and the "reds")—exhibit-
ed higher levels of self-esteem than did those who were not
assigned to any group. Other experiments showed that people
tended to see *their* random group and the people in it as better,
more likable, and more fair than the other random group. They
also tended to favor those in their own group when allocating
rewards and perceived their accomplishments as greater (even
when there was no evidence to support that point). In-group
members, unlike out-group members, remembered good actions
while forgetting bad ones. All of these factors, according to
social identity theory (Tajfel 1981), are an expression of the fundamental tendency for people to enhance their own self-esteem
by associating with groups that they believe are "better" in some
ways. People need to be "above" others.[12]

It is plausible that the enactment of a strong distinction
between labor and management creates the kind of effects
described by identity theory. As negotiators build up their sense
of in-group solidarity, separate themselves from the opponent
during negotiations, and engage in conversations of difference
during caucuses that highlight the opponents' negative qualities,
they thereby enhance their own self-esteem. As long as there is
some basic group structure (i.e., the legal definition for negotiations as a meeting of labor and management), people will ampli-

---

12. This idea is supported by studies of the impact of promotions and pay differen-
tials. Stouffer et al. (1949) and Merton (1957) discovered that what mattered to soldiers was not how well they did, but how well they did compared to those in their
"reference group." They could feel well off alone, yet experience "relative depriva-
tion" in comparison to what those around them achieved. Robert Frank (1985) has
tried to reshape economic theory around the notion of status dominance—people,
he argues, are willing to be paid less if they can be the best in a group, while they
expect to be paid a premium in order not to leave a group where they are among
the worst. People gain utility from being above others, so that social position serves
as implicit compensation.

fy these distinctions in the process of building group identity and self-respect.[13]

Difference as a Basis of Group Membership

The need to build up a group identity and create groupwide solidarity is especially important as groups are just beginning to form. When new groups form, individuals are concerned about whether they will be accepted by the group, whether their goals match those of the group, and whether they really belong (Schein 1988). During these anxious times group members are not adventuresome: They stick to known patterns, contribute in ways that are likely to produce agreement, and test new ideas in small ways before going too far out on a limb.[14] There will eventually be some competition among members for control, but as groups form, the dominant goal is inclusion and acceptance.

These dynamics are common to negotiations since bargaining is normally done by newly formed, temporary work groups. For the union, the team may include international staff representatives, elected local leaders, and shop stewards; for management, it could include line managers, staff labor relations managers, or outside council. Usually these people have not worked together

---

13. In one fascinating, albeit preliminary, study Nelson (1983) conducted a network study of the Jamestown (New York) Area Labor Management Committee. The committee, he found, helped break down the normal labor-management divide that had dominated community politics, but in its place a new set of divisions emerged. Several clusters (with no easily identifiable logic) formed. Community events were attended by members of one cluster, not the other, and views on strategies for approaching labor-management conflicts lined up according to membership in these clusters. While the particular form of the divide was changed, some division seemed to be necessary. Nelson interprets this finding in terms of Claude Lévi-Strauss's theory of duality in human cognition. It might also be interpreted as an expression of social identity theory.

14. A tendency to risk adverseness may be due to the fact that, while in-group members are usually favored more than out-group members, in-group members who stand out and are disliked actually receive more strongly negative judgments than outsiders. This is due to the fact that people care more about in-group members than out-group members (Marques, Yzerbyt, and Leyens 1988).

before, or if they have, only infrequently. During the early group meetings the problems of inclusion and acceptance are central.

In that context it is not surprising to find negotiators engaging in conversations that emphasize the negative qualities of the other side. Despite any differences among them, the one element they are certain to have in common with teammates is opposition toward the opponent. In my observations these conversations were most prominent early in negotiations, especially in the first several caucus meetings.[15] As team members got to know each other and individuals on the other side, these conversations diminished in number and strength.

Thus, on both an institutional and team or personal level, the labor-management distinction is part and parcel of creating group identity, belonging, and coordination: for each, clarifying whom they are and whom they oppose is an essential part of their ability to form a group.

Attempts to Deviate from the Pattern

Instances when the labor-management distinction was not maintained are notable. In several cases negotiators forgot the rules and were reminded of their mistakes. At the Hartford Centrum one union negotiator sat on the other side of the table during a break and forgot to move back when management returned; he was quickly and forcefully reminded, "You're on *our* side," and he moved his chair. At Northern Pigment, when one union negotiator began to explain the company's argument, the lead bargainer stopped him by joking (with a hint of seriousness), "You're taking *their* side."

In the cases where negotiators were trying mutual gains bargaining, they intended to minimize their enactment of the labor-

---

15. During the early phases of teamwork there is a tendency to stick to issues and topics that engender low levels of internal conflict (Bales and Strodbeck 1951).

management division. These efforts proved to be awkward and rarely worked. At Texas Bell negotiators from each side were supposed to work together as a team in small breakout groups during training. In the session I watched, labor and management negotiators naturally took opposite sides of the room, and after a moment of silence (no one was officially in charge), the highest ranking manager picked up the marker from the holder at the base of the flip-chart and began to lead the discussion. At Western Technologies, negotiators initially wanted to avoid sitting on opposite sides of the table. At the first meeting everyone stood around, staring at the chairs, not knowing where to sit, until the union's lead bargainer finally instructed his team to sit with him on one side of the table. And at least one MGB trainer[16] has stopped trying to get negotiators from both teams to sit interspersed; they were so uncomfortable that they were distracted from the actual training. It is important, it seems, to keep visible reminders of groupness alive.

One of the most surprising events occurred during the first days of the Midwestern University negotiations. These negotiators, trying to stick to the prescriptions of mutual gains bargaining, had been making a concerted effort not to appear as separate groups: Teams did not sit on opposite sides of tables, and caucuses were not taken during the joint meetings. Yet, during the first management meeting after the opening day of negotiations, the conversation quickly turned to differences between "us" and "them."

This meeting began slowly, with no one quite knowing how to start. I wondered, as I watched, what attitude they would take toward the union. It seemed that no one knew what to say or how others felt. The first person to break the ice complained about the union: "They had a bad case of the Rodney Dangerfield syndrome, 'We don't get no respect.'" This set the tone: It was all

---

16. Mike Gaffney, personal conversation.

right now, in private, after several hours of mutual gains bargaining, to relax and let us be us and them be them. Another complained, "We are into classic union behavior; it's all out there." One negotiator departed from the spirit of these comments, explaining that some individual union negotiators did seem quite sensible. The lead bargainer tried to focus the conversation on the tasks at hand ("We have a lot to do," he pleaded) and explained some of the union's political concerns. But after these attempts to derail the initial conversation of difference, the team broke into an open volley of anger, frustration, and descriptions of "them." "They" lacked skill, were "reluctant to take responsibility," and were engaging in "typical union behavior."

What impressed me was the ease with which the union was seen as a collective entity, a unitary "they." There were some efforts to see bargainers as individuals with particular attributes and skills,[17] and to attribute actions to context (their political concerns), but the comments were overridden by general typing of the union team as a whole, and by seeing behavior as an indicator of inherent attributes. Those who saw the other team in more subtle terms backed off and held their tongues—for a while at least—and let the conversation center on the incompetence of their collective opponent.

Although this would be a case where the labor-management distinction was kept in check during many parts of the negotiations (see chapter 9), at this point they seemed to need to create a clear sense of us versus them—and to be reassured that "we" were more right, skilled, or organized than "they" were. This need may have been heightened by the fact that overt conflict and separation into sides was dampened by the effort to apply MGB principles to bargaining. Unable to establish unambiguously the existence of the two sides during bargaining, the team

---

17. Brown (1986) reports that, without "individuating" information, people tend to see members of other groups in terms of stereotypes.

belatedly affirmed its collective identity in caucus meetings. In spite of MGB there were still two sides to bargaining.

Implications of This Division

An emphasis on the labor-management divide is useful for negotiators, as we have seen, but also has some negative implications. The addition of a little competition between groups leads members to not only build up their own group but also put down the other group (Brown 1986). This includes, in experiments, being quick to see the other group's many negative traits, choosing payoff patterns that hurt the other group more (even though that means hurting your own group as well), and even attacking the other group.[18] In terms of bargaining, these tendencies can have effects that are counterproductive. Antagonism is increased, distrust produced, and judgments about the others' positions and goals misinterpreted. Opposing teams are likely to be seen as far more homogeneous than they really are (they are seen as "all alike"), so that some interests and ideas are likely to be missed.[19] And, to the degree that group formation, status differentiation, and social identity are fundamental goods produced by the negotiation process, there exists an inherent barrier to the creation of a shared identity and common ground.

---

18. Related research—about how people make sense of the behavior they observe and the degree of blame they think others deserve for their actions—has found that people tend to be able to see the situational causes of their own actions (providing an excuse for the actions) while attributing the cause of others' actions to their own character or intentions (making it more difficult to provide any excuse) (Ross 1977). This pattern of excusing oneself and blaming the other occurs between groups as well as people.

19. Robinson, Keltner, Ward, and Ross (1992) have shown that there is a general tendency for negotiators to see their opponent's positions as more extreme than they really are. In his work with Palestinians and Israelis, Kellman (personal conversation) has found each side holding surprisingly inaccurate assessments of the other's positions on issues that are very basic to them.

While differences in interests between the two sets of people are fundamental, structuring the interactions to identify and reinforce the group distinction is likely to exacerbate any differences, make positions seem more extreme, and produce dynamics that make finding common ground even more difficult. What may drive relations between groups in negotiations is showing that one group is above the other, not maximizing joint gains or even the gains for one's own group.

Labor versus Management: A Social Construction of Reality

Most of the time the notions of "labor" and "management" remain abstractions. More often the kinds of distinctions that affect people's lives are local and concrete, such as those between a worker and a boss, or between people who work on a project together and those who do not. The more general grouping of labor and management is there to be called upon but remains inactive most of the time. When labor and management sit down to negotiate, they must make this one part of their identity the guiding element of their behavior. They know that they have to perform the role of defender of one group and opponent of the other group. In a sense the guiding principle of the negotiation performance is to display—for teammates, opponents, and constituents—a clear picture of whose side you are on.

3   Defining Roles:
Acting as Representative

Negotiators are careful to show that they are on the same side, but within each side are those who do the negotiating and those who have others negotiate for them. This role structure dominates negotiators' view of their responsibilities. On the one hand, it sets up expectations that they lead and take initiative: Negotiators have access to more information than constituents and have been delegated the authority (within bounds) to make decisions. On the other hand, it sets up expectations that they convey constituent views and gain constituents' approval: Negotiators are constrained by the desires and expectations of constituents.

These expectations often bind them: At times, when negotiators should lead their side toward compromise, fear of constituent responses may prevent compromise. At other times, when open, cooperative discussion might solve problems, fear of constituent claims of "selling out" may inhibit those discussions. And, while constituents may want each and every view to be represented, negotiators have to let some goals take precedence over others in order to make a deal. Acting as representatives (figure 3.1) is a role that places negotiators on a short leash, both substantively and behaviorally. This chapter shows how negotiators feel constituent pressures and the logic of constituents' tendency to carefully monitor their representatives.

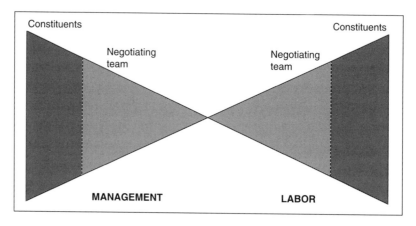

Figure 3.1
Negotiators and constituents

The Formal Organization of Constituent-Representative Relations

The constituent-representative relationship is fundamentally based on a formal structure of representation. At Midwestern University, for example, the union was made up of members and a board of directors. A bargaining council was created that included 26 faculty members who were responsible for setting general goals for negotiations and for providing negotiators with ready access to a broad cross section of member perspectives (using personal contacts and surveys). A second group, the actual bargaining team, consisted of the vice president of the union, who was automatically the lead bargainer for the union, the union's full-time staff manager, general members, and members of the union's board of directors. Thus, when the negotiators began their work, there were layers of constituents to whom they were responsible, and a dense web of ties between the union negotiators and union members.

In other cases there were more or less elaborate systems of representation. At International Harvester a bargaining council of several hundred included local chairmen and presidents and ad hoc members (the number was based on the size of the local). The local chairmen (there were 18 in 1979) made up the bargaining team, which was led by several full-time staff people from the International union. At smaller negotiations, like the Hartford Centrum, the members (about 70 people) elected stewards who automatically sat at the table as their representatives. A full-time union official from the Amalgamated local led the bargaining team.

In each of these cases the presence of constituents was felt both at the bargaining table and away from it. At IH, members talked with their representatives on the bargaining council, who were in frequent contact with the members of the bargaining team, who watched the International staff as it led the negotiations. At the Hartford Centrum, union members worked with their stewards, who represented them at the bargaining table, so information about negotiations could be readily transmitted to the membership. At Midwestern the bargaining team reported weekly to the union's board and met occasionally with the bargaining council. Constituents both watched negotiations from afar and observed negotiations from the bargaining table.

On the management side, negotiators also act as representatives of their constituent group—their bosses. They have to worry about what an immediate boss wants, what the CEO wants, and perhaps what a broader range of top- and middle-level managers want. In some cases, as in the 1990 New Bell Publishing example, the lead bargainer may create a formal bargaining council of top managers. These managers were involved in planning for negotiations and approving key decisions. Such a group helped the lead bargainer to ensure that positions taken in negotiations were broadly supported. In other cases top executives and negotiators might formally or informally survey managers before setting the company's bargaining objectives.

Occasionally negotiators had to answer only to the president of the company.

The existence of constituents—whether at the table or not—dominates bargainers' concerns. Constituents influence the goals for bargaining, affect the careers of negotiators (through political support or performance reviews), and ultimately have to approve any agreement that is reached.

Experiencing Constituents' Performance Expectations

On the positive side, constituent intransigence is a source of power. To the degree that negotiators could credibly claim that their constituents were adamant about some issue—the more irrationally, unceasingly adamant the better—they could claim that their hands were tied so the opponent had to compromise. At Western Technologies, worker anger about lump-sum payments in the last contract was so clear to union representatives that they could not possibly allow lump sums in this contract. When management tried to get the union to talk about lump sums, the lead bargainer stated honestly, "You don't need to convince us. You have to come up with something to convince those 700 people back in the plant." At the Lowell Animal Shelter the board provided their negotiators with a set budget. With worrisome income projections in hand, economic logic and sound business judgment dictated that they set a reasonable limit on wage increases. Given the strategic benefits of such constraints, it is not uncommon for negotiators to conjure up images of constituent anger or economic desperation and then act behind the scenes to ensure that constituents would not say anything to cast doubt on those images.

On the negative side, however, constituent expectations at times constrained negotiators' discretion too much and blocked innovation. It was difficult to propose new ideas and get support for anything but marginal changes or to alter unrealistic constituents' hopes. Constituent intransigence can provide power, but it can also lock negotiators into an untenable position. The lead union negotiator at the Lowell Animal Shelter realized that they were in a bind: The membership seriously expected a 12% raise when only half that amount was possible. At the Centrum, management negotiators had been sent to the table with a budget that, if not modified, would have led to a strike. And at Brick Industries the local negotiator refused to accept lump-sum payments, saying quite seriously, "They'll laugh at me if I take this back" to the membership. The international union rep knew that this attitude might unwisely throw them into a strike, so he gravely reminded the local negotiator, "We're getting down to the nitty-gritty, folks," but to no avail.

Modifying constituent positions is somewhat easier for management: Only a few people need to be convinced and, as long as their judgments are based on rational economic calculation, negotiators need only provide them with a simple cost-benefit analysis. Nonetheless, managers as well as union members have been know to commit themselves emotionally to an untenable position and become trapped in the dynamics of escalating commitment (Pruitt and Rubin 1986). One labor lawyer pointed out that owners of small businesses take it vary hard when unionized, which affects how they negotiate. A more famous example is the way that Frank Boorman, CEO of the now-defunct Eastern Airlines, allowed a personal conflict with Charles Bryan to affect his negotiations with the Machinists Union (Saunders 1992).

Just as important as these substantive expectations are constituents' expectations about the negotiation process. Constituents seem most reassured when negotiators stay distant from the other side, follow strict (unspoken) rules of procedure, and hold out until the last minute. At Midwestern University a union bargainer explained his worry about looking too cooperative early in negotiations, saying, partly tongue-in-cheek, "They [constituents] don't want us to 'sell out' until the last day." And a labor lawyer explained that some of his clients were not happy unless they saw a certain amount of "table pounding."

The strength of constituents' expectations, and the legitimacy of negotiators' fears about their reactions, was most visible in the Midwestern University case, in which the negotiators really did deviate from normal negotiating practice. (I will discuss this case in great detail in later chapters.) The kinds of constituent pressures they faced during their struggle to use the mutual gains approach illustrates many dimensions of the constituent-representative tension. Note the degree to which both substantive and behavioral expectations are part of the following story.

The Midwestern Case

Several weeks into negotiations, negotiators at Midwestern University tried to engage in open brainstorming on solutions to their problems. They wanted to explore new, unusual, or even crazy ideas without necessarily committing to any of them. They would develop as many options as possible, according to the MGB philosophy. But it turned out that constituents were not very comfortable with this process: They did not like the fact that strange ideas were being discussed, the fact that these ideas had not been censored by them, nor the fact that negotiators were acting independently of their control.

Facing Union Constituents

Unhappiness with the process burst out during a meeting between negotiators and the subset of the bargaining council that was responsible for compensation. The lead bargainer, Doug, began to tell the group about one idea for structuring compensation (called the "phase plan") that had been discussed at the main table. Harry, one of the more radical members of the council, immediately interrupted him by shouting angrily, "I never heard about this!" Doug responded, matter of factly, "It's

Ken's idea [Ken was on the union's bargaining team]; State University has a phase plan." Harry, who was indignant that negotiators were talking about ideas that his committee had not authorized, responded, "We've been chopping our gums, while you've been doing something else! Why is it coming out *now*?" Doug, trying to be positive about the phase idea began to explain, "It decompresses salary and. . . ." He was immediately cut off by Harry who shouted, "This is ridiculous!" John, a more moderate member of the council, rose to support Harry, "I've been at meetings. Ken was at only one meeting. If we don't have any influence, why meet?" Ted tried to defend Doug, "We decided early on to let the team develop options. If it's a good idea, why 'can' it?"

Negotiators went on to discuss the fact that the phase plan eliminated merit pay. Harry worried that constituents were sharply divided over merit pay and complained again about procedures and how it would look to union members:

We're going to have a heck of a problem if our constituents want to keep merit. We have no authority to cut it out. And if it matches the interests of the administration [as Doug had just argued], it makes it look like a "done deal" for the administration. And I protest the procedure—that a complicated idea is not brought to us for involvement. It is not open and sharing.

John concurred, "It does make us look funny as a subcommittee. There is not even a hint of it on the salary survey [that members filled out before negotiations]." He did not want the negotiators to take any steps beyond what was officially authorized. Susan, one of the negotiators, explained the committee's actions by pointing out, "It just evolved." She wanted them to understand that it was not *hidden* from them. She went on to remind everyone that this was just one idea that came up during the process, "There may be other options we develop at the table." Harry responded, "You'll get people angry at us. You haven't thought it through. Something so significant is hard to sell *our* people." Again he was worried about how members would react.

Part of the problem was that the pay plan inadvertently touched on an issue about which the membership was highly, and passionately, divided—the use of merit pay. After some debate over whether they had a mandate to eliminate merit pay, Ted tried to put an end to the phase plan, arguing that once an idea was considered, it could not be rescinded, "I suggest you don't put it forward. Once you put that corpse on the table, it will be impossible to push it off!"

Most of the members of the bargaining team simply watched events unfold during this meeting, saying little. The committee shot down their past efforts, while failing to provide any clear direction on key issues. Toward the end of the meeting, Doug cautioned, "It is hard for a group that meets every day to work with a group that meets once a week. It will go very fast now in negotiations. You [on the subcommittee] have to think through in 15 minutes what took us five days. It's something innate in the system."

Harry rejected the idea that the problem was "innate" to the system, and some argued that the ground rules (that bargainers would not publicly discuss ideas that were developing in negotiations) were wrong: The team had to be able to talk with the subcommittee. Most important, Harry pointed out, "*Their* [the bargainers'] ideas will get equal attention to the ideas that *we* generated." To limit such impropriety, someone suggested that if any new ideas were developed by the bargainers, they should publicize it in a newsletter and call a faculty forum. They had to be careful about public opinion. Harry concurred, adding that cutting merit pay would hurt the union, "Out there are enemies who label the AEW as 'levelers.' That's what our enemies are ready to attack us with." Another council member challenged Harry's claim, "*Some* people are upset with merit! They are sorry that the AEW is not *blocking* merit." Another council member, recognizing that no one was going to win this debate, pointed out, "We should do what we think is right. There are views on

both sides. We have to lead." Finally, Jim said, "The sad and cynical truth is that the faculty will ratify *anything* we give them!"
The real constituency problem, it appeared, was with this council and the few other faculty members who were active in the
union, not with the broader union membership.

The meeting ended. Susan and Doug walked down the hall
alone. Comparing main-table negotiations with the administration to the negotiations he had just had with members of his
own side, Doug said, *"Their* team is *easy!"*

What these negotiators were experiencing was an overriding
sense of distrust and anxiety on the part of constituents.
Constituents did not seem to have faith in the negotiators' judgment or understanding of their true goals. They carried strong
assumptions about process, such as the notion that an idea that
is discussed cannot be taken off the table. And they were particularly concerned with implicit rules of representation that
allowed them to dictate both the content and style of their negotiators. The negotiators were forced to justify their behavior:
Their actions, they claimed, followed agreed-upon procedures,
their ideas fit past union decisions and directives, and they kept
nothing from constituents intentionally, they argued.
Negotiators defended ideas, such as the phase plan, that they
had not been defending within the negotiating team. During this
meeting with constituents, the primary division shifted from the
distinction between labor and management to the distinction
between negotiators and constituents. To Harry, the negotiators
were "them." Doug and Susan left feeling very much the outsiders in their own bargaining council.

Facing Management Constituents
Later in the Midwestern negotiations, during a meeting of the
council of deans, the administration's negotiators encountered
similar difficulties. They did not face any challenges to the procedures they were using, but they did face overwhelming nega-

tive reactions to any and all union ideas, arguments, or perspectives that were reported back to the council. The deans did not seem to want to consider issues and ideas but rather to find fault with the union and knock down any ideas associated with it.

In the process of explaining and, at times, defending the union arguments, the negotiators came to be identified with the union rather then the administration. This shifting of boundaries was one that the negotiators had neither planned nor anticipated. When one dean challenged the union's notion of transferring money between schools to fund pay increases, Richard (the lead bargainer) countered, "There is a feeling in the AEW, and they are right, that some areas are well off and growing. They say, let's make this a *university*." He also told the deans that the union was being quite reasonable this year, "Look at the AEW newsletter in your packet—Grant Sacks praised the salary structure. This is a *big* change from the past." Other negotiators tried to convey the union's view, albeit with somewhat less sympathy than Richard had done. After one dean said that there should not be across-the-board raises because "there are good professors and bad professors," a negotiator reminded him, "That terminology doesn't play across the table." Another pointed out during the discussion of benefits that, "Laura [the union administrator] does not believe she can sell a co-premium. We're really down to a political question." The bargainers found themselves presenting the union's views, defending the logic of the union's arguments, and, at times, defending the union's integrity.

One of the deans worried aloud about whose side his team was representing, "I think this is a good discussion, but the tone is that *our* team is on *their* side." The deans challenged the bargainers as if they were their opponents, and the bargainers presented the union's view in a way that showed that they understood and partly identified with those views. On both the management and union sides, negotiators were eyed with suspicion and doubt and became the embodiment of the opponent. The negotiators felt rejected and constrained.

The Logic of Constituent Monitoring

Dominating the example above is an overriding sense of constituents' mistrust in negotiators. They assign individuals to act as their agents at the negotiating table but are not completely comfortable with letting them loose to get as much as possible. They insist that specific proposals be conveyed to the other side and dislike innovations—of process or content—on the part of negotiators. They watch negotiators and reprimand them if actions do not fit their expectations. Why do constituents limit negotiator flexibility in this way, and thus limit their ability to get the best deal possible? There are several components that answer this question: (1) Agents' interests may not be aligned with constituent interests, so monitoring is required; (2) constituents themselves may have multiple, conflicting interests, so monitoring is required; (3) outcomes may be difficult to assess objectively, so monitoring has to be largely "process" based; and (4) the formal processes followed by bargainers may be an intrinsic good for constituents.

Negotiators Who Serve Themselves

Constituents' most obvious concern is that negotiators have their own personal interests. At the Nebraska NBP negotiations in 1986, the union representative for the sales force was a high-performing salesman. Given his past performance, he could be influenced by management to favor a commission scheme that paid top performers like him even more while paying average performers less. As information about this type of potential change reached other salespeople, they began to worry that he would accept management's new plan based solely on the fact that *his* income would be boosted. They thought of replacing this negotiator but decided instead to add a second salesperson to the team. There were some worries on the management side as well. One negotiator had a daughter in the bargaining unit; management thought that he would give in to the union to help his family. Negotiators on both sides admitted in interviews that they played to the individual interests of opposing bargainers to influence their decisions.

Constituents also worry that negotiation professionals have too many career incentives to cooperate with the other side. At IH, operating people felt that the labor relations specialists who negotiated with the union were too concerned with getting through negotiations (and maintaining good relations with the union so their job would be easier) and too little concerned with their needs as managers. And at NBP (1990) the lead bargainer knew that some top managers expected him to "give in" to the union at the last minute and were waiting in the wings to oppose him. What he knew would be a tactically required several-day contract extension, managers would interpret as being soft on the union. More generally, constituents worry that their bargainers, after spending so much time interacting with the opponents, might be co-opted by the other side. This is a standard problem for "boundary spanners" (Adams 1976) because they are often located away from their home group, spend much time with outsiders, and have to present the views of outsiders to constituents. This was apparent at the Midwestern deans' council meeting: Negotiators spent much of their time presenting union arguments and, in the process, reinforced some deans' concerns about their bargainers' loyalties.

Intragroup Divisions

Even though negotiators may faithfully represent the interests of some constituents, they may not represent them all. As we saw in the Midwestern case, it was impossible for the negotiators to represent all views: Some faculty opposed merit pay, while others sought to destroy it; some deans were vehement that merit pay be used, while others did not care. On both the union and management sides of negotiations, there are many subgroups with different interests.

At Texas Bell the union included people with very different types of jobs (e.g., clerical workers, telephone workers, and field-based repair workers) and people from the higher-paid Houston and Dallas areas as well as from the lower-paid "small-town" areas. At NBP the union included both highly compensated, self-assertive, commissioned salespeople and the lower-income clerical workers who processed salespeople's accounts. And in every company older workers were more concerned with pension benefits, while younger ones were concerned with current wages levels.[1] In these cases each group worries that the other has too much control. At NBP clerical members worried that the sales rep on the bargaining team would dominate negotiations by virtue of his personal dominance at the table (most good salespeople can be rather domineering!), while the salespeople were concerned that the clerical workers would dominate negotiations by virtue of their larger numbers. At Texas Bell small-town locals (with only 4,000 members) complained that the Houston and Dallas locals (with over 12,000 workers) controlled the union and the negotiations. To calm their fears, two of the six union positions at the bargaining table were reserved for representatives from small-town regions, but this still left the larger city locals with the majority block on the negotiating team.

---

1. There are also conflicts between present and future workers, as occurred when American Airlines negotiated a two-tiered salary structure in 1983 (Lorsch and Loveman 1991). It was not hard to get that contract ratified since none of the people who were making the sacrifice were actually voting. Over time, however, as more of the total employee population was made up of those lower-tiered workers, it became increasingly difficult to ratify a contract that maintained the two-tiered wage differential.

On the management side, NBP was faced with a split within its ranks in 1986. The corporate marketing staff was convinced that a tougher pay-for-performance plan for salespeople would enhance the company's performance, while local managers worried that the plan would present too many managerial problems.[2] At Midwestern, the administration included deans from the wealthier schools, such as medicine, business, and engineering, and those from poorer schools, such as arts and sciences, design, and education. Each was concerned about different types of students, different patterns of grant acquisition and distribution, and different levels of dependence on schoolwide resources such as the library system. Splits within management such as these, however, were usually less visible than those on the union side; the managerial constituent group is much smaller, disagreements among them are not aired in public, and formal lines of authority enable top executives to impose a decision on negotiators if the dust has settled and they have made a clear choice.[3] As a researcher, internal management divisions became visible to me only in those cases where I had very high level of access on the management side.

The complexity of intragroup divisions makes the job of the negotiator quite difficult. One local leader at Texas Bell complained, "The problem is the membership. It is a cross section of society, from the college educated to dope shooters. We can't resolve everyone's problem." In 1986 the union negotiators at NBP had to keep enough clerical people and salespeople happy

---

2. They would have a hard time, with the new incentive system, to get people to service certain (usually large) accounts. Also, they argued, most of the work is done by average performers (almost by definition), so a system that motivated only top performers would not be best. And extreme incentives might encourage salespeople to game the system. Corporate staff thought that these managers were just trying to escape their responsibilities as managers.
3. The importance of formal authority, however, should not be overdrawn. Executive dictates were at times resisted by their negotiators; in one case the negotiators refused to offer a benefit that management wanted to give the union because the lead bargainer was angry at the union and did not want to "give" them anymore. This

to support the contract. And management's lead bargainer at NBP (1990) spent much of his time prior to bargaining trying to build a coalition in support of his bargaining plans among top executives and line managers.

Ambiguous Outcome Measures

If there were clear, unambiguous criteria against which constituents could measure the results, their distrust of negotiators would not be such a problem. If negotiators produced poor results, constituents could simply reject the agreement and, after negotiations, withhold political or professional support from those who did the poor negotiating. At times agreements are rejected and negotiators are punished, but in most cases negotiating results are not so easy to judge.

In the Western Technologies case union members were unhappy with lump-sum payments and were vocal about their displeasure. But they did not think that the results were so bad until they found out that the managers were not also getting lump-sum increases. A deal they considered good when convinced that the company could afford only lump-sum increases turned sour when they found that the company was able to fund general wage increases for managers. At HCI the union finally negotiated severance pay at a rate of three weeks pay for each year worked. Did the bargainers produce good results? If the negotiators fought hard and got as much as they could, then they got good results. If they did not fight hard and accepted a lower amount than was necessary, then they got poor results. At the Hartford Centrum Mike Ross explained that he had to take

---

action threw the negotiations into disarray for several days. More generally, to acknowledge that unions are, at their core, political organizations and thus driven by political concerns far more than management does not imply that management is apolitical (it is highly political) or that the veneer of rationality and control that is presented (Jackall 1988) is really the driving force of managerial behavior.

negotiations into mediation because it showed constituents that they had fought as hard as possible.

Management constituents may have an equally hard time evaluating results. Eric Schmertz, New York City's representative for the 1991 negotiations with the teachers' union,[4] agreed to give teachers a 5.5% wage increase. He argued that this was a good deal for the city because only 1.5% of that money came out of "city money" (the rest was funded by the teachers' pension plan). But the *New York Times* and the broader political establishment complained that he should have negotiated a wage freeze. They speculated that Schmertz did not fight hard enough because of his cooperative style and his former position as mediator for the city.

To a certain degree, performance can be evaluated against the bargaining objectives that were set before the negotiations began. But these objectives are often vague, contradictory, or based on hopes rather than clear goals, especially on the union side. At Midwestern the union's position on merit pay remained ambiguous well into negotiations. Union members at Hartford and other locations wanted the union to convey requests that they knew were not likely to be accepted; the initial set of requests that each side makes does not represent a true set of bargaining objectives. And, even though constituents know that some issues will be dropped and others kept, they may not know in advance what their true priorities are: They determine those priorities as negotiations progress and they are truly forced to make choices. For example, at HCI the union team did not initially focus on the issue of maintaining workers' disability compensation; the issue gained more prominence as negotia-

---

4. This interpretation is based on "Schmertz's Return," *Manhattan Lawyer*, March 1991, p. 4; "Praised as a Deal-Maker; Faulted as Too Diplomatic," Robert D. McFadden, *New York Times*, March 10, 1991; Schmertz's unpublished letter to the *New York Times* editor, and his presentation at the Program on Negotiation, Harvard Law School.

tions went on. The team understood better, at that time, the impact of the plant closing and its effect on accident claims. At Hartford Mike Ross had to constantly test ideas on the committee to "see how they react" during negotiations because "they don't know what they want until they're in this." Union negotiators do know the long list of demands that come from constituents, but real priorities emerge only as negotiations progress.

Managerial goals are often more concrete. Usually there is a budget for bargaining, and at times dozens of pages of planned offers, counter offers, and contingency plans. At HCI management could not afford to give too much but also worried that, if their negotiator gave the union too little, then employee relations would be damaged in the long run; the negotiator was expected to come in exactly on target. Nonetheless, management's initial positions are also filled with a "laundry list" of items that are dropped or traded during negotiations. In addition there is enough ambiguity of goals that management as well as union negotiators have to check repeatedly with line managers or top officials to clarify what they really care about and why. Final decisions are only made under pressure.

Process Monitoring

Given that constituents have reasons to mistrust negotiators, and given a lack of clear criteria for measuring output, constituents make sure that negotiators are acting properly as their representatives. They do so by monitoring (at the table or from a distance) the process as well as the results of negotiations[5]: They check to see that their requests are presented to the opposing side; they look for vigor, effort, and energy on the part of the

---

5. Walton and McKersie (1965) refer to constituent "behavioral expectations." Adams (1976) also discusses constituent observations about how friendly a boundary spanner is with the outsider he contacts.

negotiators; they listen to negotiators' statements to see that they provide reassurances of their loyalty. None of these actions actually measures the quality of the negotiators' bargaining strategy, the wisdom of their decisions about countering opponent proposals, or their skills of persuasion or problem solving; they monitor the symbols, trappings, and rituals of negotiations.[6] They do, however, provide reassurance that the bargainers are enacting their formal role as bargainers and are, superficially at least, acting in the constituents' interest and not their own, a subgroup's, or the opponents'.

Process as an Intrinsic Good

Certain elements of the negotiation process may also have intrinsic benefits to constituents, especially for the union. The very reason for the union's existence is to express member concerns, and negotiations are one time when management has to listen. In some cases it is just as important that members know that their requests are presented to management, as it is that their requests are granted by management.[7] If bargainers were to cut

---

6. The situation is like Meyer and Rowan's (1977) discussion of how we monitor school systems: In schools, the core technology (i.e., creating understanding among pupils) is not visible, and we do not know exactly how teachers create understanding. Therefore, what we monitor are the external, visible aspects of schools, such as the formal structure and the kinds of degrees held by teachers. Similarly Feldman and March (1981) have argued that organizations collect information as much to reassure observers that they are fully rational and comprehensive in their reasoning, as to actually get and use that information. DiMaggio and Powell (1983) have argued that given a lack of understanding within organizations of true cause-and-effect relations, observers attribute success or failure to organizational forms and rituals. In all of these cases we depend on external symbols and indicators in order to assess competence.

7. Merry and Silbey (1984) make the point that plaintiffs often reject mediation as an alternative to a full court hearing even though a narrow cost-benefit analysis favors mediation. The reason for this choice, they show, is the fact that people—especially those who are poor and feel little control in their lives—want to go through the full judicial process. They want to be heard as much as to win. Similarly one union negotiator in my interviews explained that in arbitrations it is often just as important to put on a good show, "working over" management for the members in the audience, as it is to win the case. What is important is being heard and putting up a fight.

out some of their constituents' requests before presenting them to management, it would eliminate their sense of influence.[8]

Following their dictates also reassures members that the union is in fact *their* representative, and reaffirms that the union is democratically structured, with leaders serving only at the behest of its members. Given this purpose, there is no legitimate basis for negotiators to omit member proposals from their list of demands, and as individual requests are dropped or modified, the process has to be open and fair. At Midwestern, Harry was very concerned that the procedure be a very open and democratic one. He worried not only about the specific content of ideas developed at the table but the fact that the ideas were developed by bargainers rather than by the members of the bargaining council.

In response to these pressures, the traditional negotiation process includes behaviors that reassure constituents that negotiators are acting as their representatives at the bargaining table; the traditional process includes rituals of representation in addition to rituals of opposition.

Leading and Following

Conflicting Role Requirements

The constituent role pressures just discussed, taken to the extreme, define a role for negotiators as conduit of information: Negotiators collect constituent requests and present these to the other side, responses are duly recorded and conveyed back to constituents, and constituents provide the negotiator with new instructions. As Jeff Moore, the company's lead bargainer at

---

8. On the management side, negotiator representation of constituent views is not so much of an intrinsic benefit. Top management officials have an ongoing direct influence in the operations of the company—they do not depend on negotiations to have a sense of "voice."

HCI, explained to the union at one point, "I am a courier. I take my directions. I take information." Many members of bargaining teams see their role only in such narrow terms and act, in effect, as constituents sitting at the bargaining table. But at the same time negotiators have to play a more proactive role. When there are ambiguous objectives and contending factions, it is not possible for negotiators to simply present constituent views. If proposals are contradictory—such as asking to eliminate merit pay and asking that merit pay be increased—they cannot both be put on the table. More typically, as negotiations progress, negotiators have to make choices between contending priorities. When the bargainers begin to make these necessary trade-offs, whether they like it or not they are no longer just conveyors of constituent views but shapers of them. As a bargaining council member at Midwestern finally acknowledged, irreconcilable differences among the union's membership was forcing the negotiators to take on a leadership role.[9]

Negotiators also have to lead if they are to gain the respect of the opponent. Opposing negotiators become highly frustrated when the negotiators they face do not shape and trim constituent proposals. Early in the Midwestern negotiations the administrative team felt frustrated that the union was doing no more than making "raw pronouncements" from their constituents. If the negotiators are not at least partly in control of their side's agenda, the opponent has little incentive to deal with them seriously. Several negotiators explained that the hardest times occurred when they had to deal with negotiators who had no authority. One management lawyer complained:

Some of the newer unions tend to be more democratic, which makes it more difficult because you can't accommodate everybody's demands. I often hope that the union leader will show a little leadership—just as I

---

9. According to Cyert and March (1963), most of organizational decision making is a process of building coalitions. People have goals, they point out, while groups do not. Goals evolve from a process of learning, bargaining, and coalition building.

know it is my responsibility to lead my clients, I look to the union rep to lead his or her client.

Thus negotiators know that they have not only to convey constituent proposals but also to help constituents become more targeted, clear, and realistic in their goals. They have to help their side learn relevant facts that emerge from the negotiations, understand when an issue will require a strike, and reorder priorities based on that information and a constant reevaluation of their own goals. In addition they have to continually forge a coalition in support of negotiations. They cannot simply present their side's views because there is no such thing. Both their "side" and "its" views are created from the negotiation process itself.

The tension between leading and following constituents is especially strong for union bargainers. Given the importance of representation as an intrinsic good for the union, they face very strong process expectations from constituents; at the same time, that democratic aspect of unions can easily reveal contending factions, create an excess of demands, and build unrealistic expectations so that more leadership is also needed. It takes a deft hand to keep up appearances as followers of members' dictates, while at the same time leading them to achieve a more focused set of goals. The tension is also especially strong for lead bargainers; as the individuals with formal responsibility for the negotiations, more experience, and greater contact with the opponent, they are under greater pressure to lead. As we will see in the next chapter, this places additional performance demands on lead bargainers; to maintain control, they have to convince others that they are leaders who deserve to be given the kinds of discretion and control that they need. The representative role is a complicated one, requiring accommodation to constituents, substantive and behavioral expectations, while also demanding initiative and the making of difficult choices.

The Art of Representational Leading

The dynamics studied in this chapter should make absolutely clear that negotiations are not a process in which there are two actors, each with a clear set of preferences, who meet across the bargaining table to reach a compromise. Rather, each side has multiple, ambiguous goals, which negotiators have to discover, focus, shape, and reshape over the course of bargaining. Borrowing from the language of business strategy, the negotiators' decision-making process is one of "logical incrementalism" (Quinn 1980) not an all-knowing strategist (Andrews 1980). Initially negotiators simply present constituent requests, acting as pure representatives. Then, after hearing the opponent's response and being sure that constituents know of that response, they turn inward, helping their side to slowly change, focus, and shape its initial requests, and helping a new set of collective expectations to slowly emerge. Those modified views are then conveyed to the other side, and the process is repeated again. Negotiators go through an ongoing process of questioning and prodding inside their group, while presenting those continually developing views to the other side. They simultaneously lead and are led by constituents. This process might appropriately be called "representational leading," to capture both the leadership element of the negotiating role, as well as some of the constraints placed on negotiators by constituents.

4   Taking Charge: Acting Like a Lead Bargainer

Among all of the negotiators it is the lead bargainers who have responsibility for managing the details of the negotiations and ensuring that the bargaining strategy is followed: They have to get the team to act as a unit, make sure that constituent pressures are managed in the right way, and ensure that plans are not revealed. This requires a certain amount of control: Team members are told what should happen and what they should or should not say. In some cases the lead bargainers control negotiations by virtue of their formal authority. In many cases, however, formal authority is limited, so control depends on their ability to convince others to follow them because of their superior skill, knowledge, and experience. Lead bargainers have to act like leaders and get the team to accept that act, in order to effectively manage the negotiation process (see figure 4.1).

The Need for Control

The essence of bargaining strategy, as it is traditionally understood, is to manipulate information and impressions. Negotiators on each side try to convince negotiators on the other side that they absolutely positively have to get a certain amount and will not settle for less, either because the request is reasonable and justified, or because they have no choice: Constituents

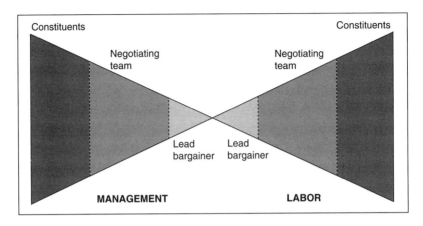

Figure 4.1
The role of lead bargainer

expect it, they have made public promises to get it, or they are committed to some principle. If such a story can be convincingly maintained, then opponents will believe that they have to make a choice between compromise and a strike. Assuming that a strike is usually more costly for the opponents, they will be forced to compromise.

This strategy depends on very tight control over information and the behavior of team members during negotiations. If one team finds out that some or all of the opponent's negotiators are willing to settle for less, or would not risk much in order to push for the higher amount, then the team would not feel pressure to compromise. To maintain pressure, it is critical that the opponent hears only one story, sees the team members acting in support of each other, and does not hear any internal doubts or debates.

But shows of unity and control over information do not always happen naturally. Each team member is likely to have at least some differences regarding priorities, degree of commitment on any given issue, and willingness to risk a strike. Lead bargainers therefore try to control their teams. Sometimes they give explicit instructions to teammates about how to act in nego-

tiations: The lead bargainer at Connecticut Hospital, we saw in chapter 2, gave her team lines to say and told them to nod in agreement with statements made by teammates; during the HCI negotiations Jeff Moore told me to be careful not to show any emotions that might reveal to the union what management had planned in caucus. At other times lead bargainers let teammates speak only briefly on very limited topics so that nothing unexpected can be said or revealed. On a more subtle level lead bargainers control their team's behavior by making sure that all team members see the situation in the same way: They interpret for the team the meaning of the opponent's actions, explain what steps are normal in negotiations, and tell them what is typical in other contracts in the region. In these ways it is possible to manage the team's emotions; they learn when the opponent's actions are a problem worth getting angry over or only a routine event that should be ignored. By coordinating the team's perceptions, emotions, and behaviors, lead bargainers gain the strategic advantage that comes from control over information and impressions.

Lead bargainers' control has other benefits as well. First, it important not only to control what the opponent sees and hears but also to control what constituents see and hear. If constituents are convinced that their representatives are acting appropriately, they are likely to give their negotiators more room to maneuver. Second, centralized control quickens intrateam decision making. At many points in negotiations, especially as the contract deadline nears, negotiators have to make decisions very quickly. Such decisions, open to democratic control, can be very slow in coming. At Midwestern University the union team bogged down in endless internal debates over merit pay. In experimental studies groups made decisions faster if there was centralized control over the flow of information (Bavales 1950). Democracy has a time and place, but so too does the use of a strong hand. Third,

control provides the bargainers with some degree of predictability. If negotiators can cut off unplanned comments by team members, shape their reactions, and control the tactics, they have less
to worry about and can concentrate on strategic decisions and
the opponent's reactions. Given that negotiators have only a limited capacity to calculate,[1] successful decision making requires
that information processing demands be contained in some way.
The lead bargainers' control makes this possible.

Formal Authority as a Source of Control

Formal authority, the unique access to information and decision
rights that comes from one's position, is one base of bargainers'
control.[2] The sources of influence associated with formal authority include (1) the right to make a decision unilaterally, (2) unique
contacts with those of higher authority who have decision-making power, (3) the ability to influence team-member career
progress outside of bargaining, and (4) unique access to decisions about the group's goals and objectives. This type of influence is not uncommon among company negotiators. In two
cases the lead bargainer for management was a vice president
for human resources. In each case the lead bargainers' sense of
control was nearly absolute, as was team deference to their judgments.

At Texas Bell Dan Hallin, the lead negotiator, had a very
strong presence. When he was in the room, his subordinates

---

1. In the words of March and Simon (1958), lead bargainers are "boundedly" rational. Given that it is beyond the capacity of people to fully analyze all of the information related to all conceivable options at any given decision point, they can only act
in a rational, adaptive way when many factors are taken as given. Thus they are
rational only within bounds.
2. One of the most dominant typologies of influence and power is that of French and
Raven (1959). Their "reward power" and "coercive power" are part of what I call formal authority. Their "referent power" is part of what I will later describe as influence
through confidence. We both identify expertise as a source of influence.

deferred to him. When he was not there, they worried about him. Staff members who were bold and outspoken in most situations became nervous and silent when he arrived. In planning meetings with the union, there were whispers that the company representatives had to succeed at being "joint" with the union because that was what Hallin wanted; during negotiations management subcommittee members asked the union to produce a joint statement of interests with management because they needed to deliver what Hallin expected. Throughout training and negotiations, he kept a tight rein on what his team did and said. He refused to allow the two sides to switch roles in a negotiation simulation because he could not then control what the "managers" in the role plays would say, and he briefed his subordinates on what to say when they played their roles in the simulation. Hallin was absolutely in charge of the negotiation process.

At Western Technologies the company's lead bargainer, Dave Henders, had a similar level of authority and a similar level of control. When he attended negotiations, he was the center of attention, and all other managers deferred to him. During much of the negotiations he let Tom Burger lead and did not attend the meetings himself. But in the final weeks he rejoined the discussion. During management caucuses at those times, team members would mill around until Henders spoke. When Henders began to talk, everyone else would be quiet and form a semicircle around him. Toward the very end of negotiations he showed up with a corporate lawyer at his side and several flip charts to point at. When he talked, he was not questioned or challenged.

For both Hallin and Henders, their job was to get an agreement. They were the only ones on the team with critical information about corporate spending limits, they had the authority to make decisions, and they were the bosses of many team members. Their staff members on the team were there for support—they did not have any independent base of authority.

Lead bargainers for the union rarely have such complete formal authority. Union members hold the ultimate decision-making authority, and the negotiators are usually elected representatives of the membership; their careers depend on satisfying members, not the lead bargainer. Labor lawyers on the management side and management negotiators who are not so high in the company's hierarchy also do not have such complete formal authority. They do have access to the managers who have formal authority, but like the union leader, they do not have the unique right to make decisions and have no influence over the careers of other team members. For these bargainers, control depends more on expertise than formal authority.

Expertise as a Source of Control

In cases where formal authority is weak or nonexistent, lead bargainers can gain control by showing others on the team that they are skilled negotiators who should be allowed to control negotiations by virtue of their expertise. Expertise is established by displaying:

1. Knowledge of the bargaining process. In almost all negotiations the lead bargainer can tell the others the true meaning of the opponent's actions and what they can expect next, enhancing their status as the "experts."

2. Knowledge of the particular opponent. Familiarity with opponents and knowledge of their particular habits and tendencies is an additional source of expertise.

3. A pattern of past successes. If negotiators have negotiated successful contracts in the past, they are deemed to be competent and therefore given a great deal of control over the team's decisions.

Expertise is highly correlated with formal position: Only those who have led negotiations before are likely to be familiar with the negotiation process and opponents' habits or have a track record of past successes, and it is likely that those who have jobs with a great deal of authority, such as Hallin and Henders, arrived at their lofty positions in part by convincing others of their status as expert bargainers. But expertise is conceptually distinct from formal position: Those who are lead bargainers may not have any experience or may not be able to convince teammates that they deserve respect as experts, and there may be team members who are not lead bargainers but have enough experience to be experts. To establish their role as experts, lead bargainers must have bargaining experience, display those skills and knowledge for others to observe, and show that their level of experience and skill is greater than that of others on the team.

Labor Lawyers as Experts

In the cases where management or the union are represented by lawyers, the lawyers' control comes from their role as technical expert. They tell clients when to weed out minor issues, how quickly to make concessions, and how to respond to opponent requests. They also tell the client how to phrase its proposals to protect itself legally, and what defenses to maintain in the contract language.

At HCI the lawyer, Jeff Moore, made sure that the management representative made his statements in exactly the right way. During the first meeting, for example, Dave Hunter, the plant manager, explained to the union that the company was planning to close the plant by March 1, but it could take until the end of April to finish the process. Moore intervened to restate management's position: The plant would surely close by April, but layoffs might begin as early as March. He did not want to let the union think that the date of the closing was open-ended. After a few more days of negotiating, Moore told Hunter that it was time to clear away all the minor issues so that they could deal with the main problem of severance pay. And, after Hunter cautioned Moore that his draft language on who would pack the plant's equipment for shipping did not respond to the union's concerns, Moore replied, "They can balk. Let them come back to us with the language." He had strategic concerns in mind.

Peter Grahame, a lawyer and lead management negotiator for the Animal Shelter, was the technical expert who decided how to conduct the negotiations. He also looked out for management's legal interests: He made sure, for example, that any new clauses in the contract would not restrict "management's rights." Management deferred to Grahame on most issues of negotiating strategy and legal content. In the cases where management was represented by outside council, the lawyer was the lead strategist and technical expert who worked closely with one or two managers. These managers informed the lawyers of their goals, but otherwise they sat quietly to the side during negotiations and let the lawyers take charge.

The Union Bargaining Expert

Union lead bargainers also control negotiations by establishing their status as negotiating experts. The union bargaining team at the Centrum included five employees, each of whom were elected to be stewards by some segment of the work force (e.g., set-up workers, the janitorial staff, or part-time workers). Most had been through negotiations before and knew Mike Ross, the lead bargainer and negotiating pro from the international union. He had negotiated contracts for them for years, so they knew what to expect from him and had faith in his abilities.

Ross kept firm control over the team, even though he encouraged input from them. At the beginning of the first meeting with management, he initiated what I learned was his standard starting ritual. He sat in the center seat at the table, opposite the door, signaled the others to sit on either side of him, folded his hands on the table, looked slowly to his left and right, and, once everyone was quiet and staring at him, asked, "Who's going to get them?" He was in charge of his team, and he wanted the management team members to see that he was the leader when they walked into the room.

After that day's negotiations, while management was leaving the room, Ross told me that his philosophy was to let the people on his team say whatever was needed, except at the end of negotiations when they were talking about money. He then turned to his team members as they were settling down and proceeded to interpret for them what had just occurred. Neal Dobie (the site manager) was taking the lead, he explained, while John Garofano (the corporate executive who was visiting for the negotiations) was not likely to return. Garofano, he elaborated, wanted to open the contract so that he would know the negotiators, which would help him to "come down at the end like a superman to close the deal." Dobie, he added, was surely "under some heat" with Garofano watching. He showed his teammates that he understood what was happening far better than anyone else (even though his belief that Garofano would leave was wrong). On the substance of management's response to their proposals, he pointed out that some issues that were rejected were not really rejected: By asking questions about an issue after rejecting the union proposal, the company was signaling that it was willing to talk about it. He was worried that their medical plan was under attack, but thought that management did not "know how strong to be against the 100% health plan."

During the following days, the pattern was set. Bargaining team members contributed occasionally, but Ross dominated the negotiations and interpreted for them during caucuses. With his interpretations, Ross conveyed the impression that he knew much more than the rest of the team about what was happening. He knew the tricks of the trade, knew when to be worried, and knew what was typical in contracts in the region that year. The one person on the bargaining team that Ross paid special attention to was Glenn. He was new to bargaining, had some personal grievances that were bothering him, and represented a key constituency—the part-time setup workers. Ross needed to make sure that Glenn was happy with the negotiations, felt his interests represented, and gained some confidence in Ross's negotiating abilities.

A few weeks later, when negotiations seemed to stall, Ross told the committee in caucus, "I don't see any movement. We're headed to an impasse. I'm gonna go talk with Garofano and say our position hasn't changed. Why don't we go for mediation?" He then left the room to talk with Garofano. Sitting with the rest of the union team members, I was struck by how uninvolved and unconcerned they were with the negotiations. Most of the talk was about personal issues and sports. Except for Glenn, they seemed to understand that a game was being played, that it was up to Ross to decide the moves, and that much would occur in private between Ross and Garofano. When Ross returned, he reported: "I said [to Garofano] 'Obviously you're not ready to settle. What does it take to settle? Our team saw your proposal for what it is. Do you want to get a mediator? It does wonders.' I don't think he has any problem with that. Mediation is standard procedure anyway."

Throughout the negotiations, Ross engaged in ongoing interpretation and commentary for his team. After management's first proposals he was able to tell his team what those proposals really meant, whether they were normal and expected, and what would come next. When an outside manager appeared at the table, he was able to explain why the man was there and what his role would be. When negotiations became difficult, he knew that it was routine to bring in a mediator. Day by day he let his team members know what was happening, what would occur next, and whether or not they were on track to achieve their goals. He knew the signals, the people, the moves, the laws, the process, and the trends. He showed that it took an expert to understand what was happening, and that he was just such an expert.

In this case we see a lead bargainer who had vastly more experience and far more influence over the direction of negotiations than others on the team. Ross was in charge, expected to be in charge, and his team members readily allowed this differential of influence. He had to defer to others at times—the negotiations were, after all, about their employment contract—but he was the unquestioned leader. He had some formal authority as the international rep, but his real influence came from his ability to convince others that he was a bargaining expert.[3]

Control through Confidence

Whether backed by formal authority or not, lead bargainers solidified their influence by enacting their role with absolute confidence. In the Centrum case Ross was cool and professional, making judgments quickly and with ease. His role and his lines were deeply familiar to him. He was in control of the situation because he was in control of himself. At Texas Bell Hallin maintained a similar veneer of self control, showing that he knew exactly what he wanted and harboring no doubts that this was

---

3. Kolb (1985) makes a similar point about labor mediators. Since they have no formal authority and no technical credentials, they have to convince others that they are knowledgeable experts: "Much of their influence stems from the expressive management of their expertise, their rapport with the parties, and the parties' perceptions of their contributions to progress and settlement in the current case and in others external to it. In the ways mediators manage these facets of their professional work, they seek to influence the parties to believe certain things about themselves and the process" (p. 23).

what he could get. Whenever either walked into a room, they waited until others stopped what they were doing and listened to them. Both physically and conversationally they put themselves at center stage, signaling their dominance. They were the ones who spoke first, initiated new ideas, and displayed their knowledge of the laws and the bargaining process. It was clear to both teammates and opponents that they were in charge. As Collins (1975) pointed out, it is through differences in interpersonal confidence that social structures are enacted and reproduced at the more micro level of social interaction.

Maintaining Control: The Importance of Process

Lead bargainers' control, we have seen, is not simply a matter of formal authority. Control comes from acting in control and performing well in the role. It is possible for challengers to emerge if there are other team members with personal confidence, bargaining experience, and/or some legitimate claim to authority. This is most likely to occur on the union side, since the lead bargainer's formal authority is limited, and it is most likely to occur in large bargaining units where team members are full-time union leaders with bargaining experience and an ability to lead. But overt challengers are relatively rare: Lead bargainers can usually adjust their performance to match the challengers', and more important, there is usually not much interest in opposing the lead bargainer. Most negotiators seem to expect and want the lead bargainer to take control.

New negotiators in all of the cases looked to the "old hands" for guidance and seemed happy to give them a large amount of influence over strategic choices. Given the ambiguity of negotiations and the amount that was at stake, few neophytes wanted to be responsible for mistakes or missteps. Experienced team members also seemed happy, in many cases, to let lead bargainers have control, since they understood that centralized control had strategic benefits. Acceptance of a leader's control is quite natural in any task group: It should not be surprising that negotiating teams also accept leadership control. In experiments on group functioning (Bales and Slater 1955) leaders always emerge: It is a fundamental need of any group and an essential part of effective group functioning. When other team members gain control over the negotiation process, it is often the result, not the cause, of a lead bargainer's failed performance.

A greater threat to lead bargainers' control is a change in the negotiation process. Much of the lead bargainers' authority comes from being experts in the process and feeling calm and confident in their ability to manage that process. To give a skilled performance, the lead negotiators have to be able to control their own stage and provide themselves with the necessary props. In the IH case, discussed in a later chapter, lead bargainers lost control because the opponent intentionally undermined the known process. In the Western Technologies case the threat was more innocent: Labor and management both had decided to use a new process of bargaining with which the lead bargainer was not familiar or skilled. As a result Hayes, the union's lead bargainer newly assigned from the international union, entered the negotiations with almost no levers for control. To begin with, he had very little formal authority: He could not affect the careers of other team members, and since Western was not part of a larger set of negotiations, he had no unique access to larger strategic plans. Authority would have to come from expertise. But he had no track record with this local and did not know the management opponents. The only advantage he had was his knowledge of the process and the confidence that would give him. But this was diminished by the decision to use the MGB process with which he was not familiar. To achieve control, he gradually shifted the negotiation process back to the traditional one that he knew. With that switch accomplished, he was the most skilled; he knew what to expect, and he could be the one to inform the team what was happening.

The Risks of Excess Control

Just as it is natural that groups have leaders, we also know that in most groups alternative leaders also emerge, sometimes oriented to different needs of the group. If one leader drives the group to accomplish its task, another might help the group achieve its sense of social unity (Bales and Slater 1955). A lead bargainer may not be able to prevent the emergence of other leaders and indeed may not want to prevent their emergence. Some shared leadership can help the team, and make the lead bargainer's job easier and more effective.

Lead bargainers' control is also likely to be inhibited by team members' expectations. They too feel a responsibility to fulfill their assigned role and thus to engage in "bargaining." They are representatives for a constituency and have to carry through their obligation to protect that constituency. They cannot let the lead bargainer take complete control, lest they and their interests be left out. If they feel that they are part of a faction that is not represented by the lead bargainer, gaining influence will be even more important. And, on the union side, it is the team members who have to answer to the membership, not the lead bargainer.

Finally, many negotiators are likely to have an inherent desire to make a contribution and have some influence. Being kept out of the loop can be frustrating, insulting, or simply boring. At Midwestern University one administration negotiator was extremely unhappy with himself and the process until he was in a subcommittee that allowed him to have some influence and control. At NBP several management negotiators became totally disengaged from the process once they realized that they were being ignored. If the lead bargainers' control is taken to the extreme, others are likely to tune out, or resist being shunted aside.

The Dramatic Basis of Control

The concentration of power in the hands of the lead bargainer has distinct advantages for negotiators: It helps them hide information, maintain a show of unity, make quick decisions, and simplify the situation so that strategic decisions can be considered. Lead bargainers strive to maintain this control and in most cases team members give it to them.

But maintaining control is not always easy. Except when lead bargainers have strong formal authority, control depends on the delivery of a performance: Lead bargainers have to act their roles. They have to show that they are experts who are comfortable as lead bargainers and confident in their skills. Even those who do not depend completely on performance as the basis of their control try to stay in role, reassuring teammates that they know what they are doing and are in charge.

Lead bargainers therefore abide by an additional layer of performance expectations beyond those discussed in the last two chapters. They worry not only about showing whose side they are on and playing the role of the representative but also about acting as a lead bargainer; they participate not only in rituals of opposition and rituals of representation but also in rituals of expertise and control. And, a successful performance requires that they make a concerted not only effort to perform the expected role but to reinforce conditions that allow them to stay in role: They strive to enact a negotiation process with which they are familiar—one that allows them to display their knowledge, skills, and expertise. The first step toward acting like lead bargainers is to show teammates that their way of bargaining is both effective and normal. Lead bargainers have to create the platform for their own performance.

5   Front Stage
and Backstage

The main table of labor negotiations is a public stage, where negotiators are highly visible: With opponents, teammates, and constituents watching, they have to carefully control what they do and say (see figure 5.1). In support of distributive bargaining strategies, little information is shared with the opponent, and each side postures to show how tough it can be. At the same time this tough facade is a way of meeting audience expectations. Negotiators have to act like opponents, representatives, and experts, showing that they are ideologically aligned with teammates and constituents, willing to push hard to achieve constituent goals, and constantly in control. Even though negotiations include both integrative and distributive elements, as Walton and McKersie[1] have pointed out, audience expectations and the group dynamics of negotiations limit negotiators to display only the distributive side of negotiations in public. On the public stage, anger and opposition dominate; rituals of opposition, representation, and control produce a drama of conflict.

At the same time there are mechanisms for private understanding between opposing lead bargainers, such as signaling

---

1. The distinction between integrative and distributive bargaining is also central to Lax and Sebenius's (1986) analysis. They emphasize that the tactics for the two approaches are in many ways contradictory; this contradiction represents the "negotiator's dilemma."

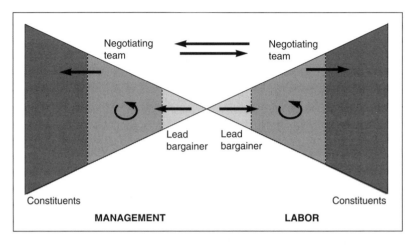

Figure 5.1
Audience structure for main-table negotiations. Arrows indicate the audiences
toward which negotiators orient their public displays. The circular arrows indicate
that members of negotiating teams perform for each other.

and sidebar discussions. Each of these mechanisms provide
ways for negotiators to communicate information while still
maintaining the drama of conflict. They occur within a social
space that is less visible to the audiences. It is here, away from
the front stage, that much of the integrative aspects of negotiations occur. But, just as the front-stage strategies of unity and
control depend on negotiators' abilities to manage their relationships with teammates and constituents, these strategies depend
on the lead negotiators' abilities to manage their relationship
with the opposing lead negotiators. And just as public drama
depends on loyalty to a particular set of negotiation rituals, so
too do the backstage communications.

Front Stage Drama of Conflict

On both the company and union sides of the negotiating table,
negotiators feel pressure to act tough. As one corporate lawyer

explained: "Some companies want table-pounding bargainers. They don't think you've done your job unless you've made some kind of noise." Another concurred: "Negotiations is highly emotional. Firms always feel like they have 'lost.' It's a very personal service to employers—like divorce law." And a union rep pointed out that "the company guy—the labor relations guy—postures for his own group—he goes back after bargaining to present himself to management."

Union negotiators were often more direct about their need to perform. One said that a good union negotiator adds the radicals to the bargaining team and then puts on a show for them; these radicals will cooperate "once they see the process and see the yelling and screaming that you are doing, and how you work management over—even if it is for show." A union lawyer told a similar story: "The client has to believe in me. They watch me very carefully. I have to negotiate effectively and make the committee *believe* that I negotiate effectively. Which may be different." As another union rep explained: "As long as the people felt good about the process it almost does not matter what we ended up with." The union rep who put radicals on his committees added:

There is a lot of show. My guys love it. I have had arbitration cases where I will bring in 25 guys and put the show on, and they don't remember I lost the case. They remember I worked over management.

Getting members to be happy about the results is largely a matter of good theater—of enhancing confidence in the bargainer and using tensions to good effect. One union lawyer criticized a union rep who insisted on giving the tentative contract to the rank and file five days ahead of the actual vote:

I think that is unacceptable. It disturbs the dynamic tension of negotiations—the climax of excitement. It is important to the rank-and-file to feel good about the contract. They want the opportunity to feel that they fought to the end, to gain dignity and respect. If they study it, they dwell on the negative. If they get it "hot off the press," they are excited.

Not only do negotiators have to maintain their image as tough fighters, they also have to be careful not to be seen as co-opted by the opponent. While most union reps and lawyers knew it was important to work *with* their counterparts, they worried about how far they could go before they lost the trust of their team and constituents. One union rep who likes to work cooperatively with management said that her members did not want "someone who screams and yells and pounds the table" if it did not get them anywhere. "But," she added, "there is a reputation that goes beyond what happens at the bargaining table. Kind of an undercurrent of 'she is easy to get along with' that you don't want said about you. It is OK to have a reputation of someone who is easy to talk to and who keeps the process going, but it is not OK to have the reputation of being easy to deal with if it means you are selling out your member's interests. *That is a very fine line there.*"

Negotiators were worried about their credibility, that of their committee, and the *impressions* that constituents had of their efforts and the agreement that they produced. These forces are especially strong for union negotiators, given a greater ambiguity of goals, their dependence on member mobilization as a source of power, and their need to respond to the political processes inherent in union organizations. These pressures and expectations lead bargainers to put on, as a company lawyer put it, "a certain amount of show."

One example of how these pressures can drive negotiators to act in a highly antagonistic way across the bargaining table comes from the HCI negotiations. The union's lead bargainer, Alan Hutchinson, abruptly shifted from being even-keeled and reasonable during main-table negotiations, to yelling at the management negotiators and proclaiming how angry he was with them. Prior to this outburst, Hutchinson seemed to be losing control to Scott Gilbert, the politically powerful and angry union vice president from the plant who had been repeatedly accusing the company of one or another attempt to "block" the union.

On that day Gilbert threatened to rescind an agreement that they had reached to shift the negotiations to days when management's lawyer, Jeff Moore, could attend. This move angered Moore, who in turn suggested to Hutchinson that, as professionals, they both knew that this was not how negotiations worked. With everyone confused and irritated, they broke into caucuses. Needing to clarify a point, Moore went to talk with Hutchinson but returned quickly reporting, "They're yelling at each other— you can hear it from the hallway." When negotiations resumed Hutchinson's attitude changed dramatically. He started, calmly: "There have been rumors from management. This is hard enough without rumors. Tell your guys to shut up, Dave." At this point, his voice grew louder, his jaw tightened, and his glare became sharper: "After December 31, the plant's closed. We're *gone*. We're not negotiating anything but what affects the community after the close-down." Moore countered: "There is no need to yell at me," but Hutchinson responded: "I am not yelling. But I have a problem negotiating COLA, shit like that, when you're closing down the plant. [more angry] It's just *not* going to happen!" After several more minutes of yelling, the union team stomped out of the room, slamming the door. Dave Hunter, the plant manager, asked Moore what was going on. Moore replied, calmly: "They're basically asking to extend the contract as is. Alan is trying to do the 'angry talk,' rather than Scott. It keeps it under control. Alan's behavior is standard. The problem is Scott."

Hutchinson was forced to take a more emotional stance toward the company in order to reassure his team—especially Gilbert—of his commitment to their goals and of the energy that he would apply to achieving them. Hutchinson's ability to direct the negotiations in productive ways and remain the leader of his team depended on "standing tough" against management. He had to enact his position as opponent of management, representative of union members, and skilled leader of the negotiations.

Mechanisms for Private Understanding

Discounting the "Act"

In the HCI example Moore, management's bargaining pro, did not take Hutchinson's act too seriously. Moore knew that Hutchinson's behavior was intended for another audience, *discounted* the act, and attributed it to other factors—in this case, the need to act like a "leader" and "opponent." Hutchinson's behavior was "normal," he told his management teammate.

This process of discounting the negotiator's performance is common. In many situations experienced negotiators know to perceive as *un*important, actions that are ostensibly important. They attribute the action not to the actor but to some contextual factor that drives the actor.[2] At International Harvester a labor relations manager, aware of the union's political dynamics explained: "[Local leaders] get their jobs by convincing their voters, the members of the union, that their predecessors had been soft on the company—which is a long way from the truth—but obviously in any political campaign, they get that kind of stuff." These managers had therefore come to expect and discount a large degree of fiery language from local union leaders and a certain amount of playing to the local leaders by top UAW negotiators. One labor relations manager at IH explained that if you take the rhetoric at face value—if you "don't understand the rituals [and instead] . . . see trivia as serious, you can make some

---

2. Most people tend to see how their own behaviors are influenced by contextual forces but miss those forces when interpreting the behaviors of others. This mistake is called the "fundamental attribution error" (Ross 1977). This example shows that lead bargainers are able to avoid this bias when dealing with each other, perhaps because they are in similar situations with such overpowering contextual forces.

very big mistakes." His job was to know how much to discount union displays: "It wasn't important whether I agreed with [the union negotiators], it was just important that I listen to them. I'd evaluate, first, how much of it was 100%, how much of it was 50%, or how much of it was 25% for effect, and then we'd discuss it in our negotiation committee meeting."

Both sides knew not to read too much into any outbursts of anger. As one IH union leader explained:

Hell, I've had management cuss me, and vice versa. That's kind of part of it. When you get hot, you let it fly. It's nothing that really sticks. Later you may have a drink with the same guy, talk about your kids or whatever.

There was a realization that this was all part of the game. One manager at IH mentioned that he hoped no one ever took too seriously the things he said across the table during debates ("You always end up saying things across the table that you wish you could take back later") and appreciated it when people took those statements for what they were: emotional outbursts and no more.

Negotiators also knew to discount the list of proposals made at the beginning of negotiations. One local leader at IH said: "Obviously, in negotiations, you went in there and threw a ten pound list of demands across the table. They obviously knew that you weren't serious about every one, that you would settle for a fraction of the items." Indeed company negotiators *did* know that the laundry list was not to be taken seriously. As a company lawyer explained:

Unions typically come in asking for the moon. They meet, people say "I want this or that," and the union leadership knows some are not realistic. But the membership says, "Why don't you ask for it." They are obligated to ask, even though management will turn them down flat. Same with management. It would be nice to take this back or that back. Nothing ventured, nothing gained.

We can see from these quotes that not only is much of the "act" of bargaining discounted, it is *expected* to be discounted.

Were opponents to take these behaviors at face value, it would create trouble: They might become angry in return or misunderstand the negotiator's position. In this way the performance is a joint act: The negotiator can play his role only if the opponent also knows it and abides by the established script. The more the negotiator can depend on the opponent's discounting of his actions, the more free he is to give a good performance.

Signaling

The flip side of ignoring what is said is hearing what is *not* said. While there are times that the negotiator needs to say things for dramatic effect, knowing that they will be ignored, there are times that the drama restricts the negotiator from saying things that need to be communicated. While the negotiator is expected to fight hard for all of the constituents' positions and maintain the role of "negotiator-in-conflict," at some point he or she has to make concessions or let the other side know the true priorities. This tension is managed by sending signals. For example, the union "will highlight those things they want us to address, without giving anything away or dropping it," explained one company lawyer.

The signals are usually well understood. Another lawyer explained:

> For a union negotiator to say, "At this time we are unprepared to drop that issue" is a clue to me that at the right moment, they will drop that issue. Or, if the response to the wage offer is, "That is all well and good but we want an additional holiday and we want to improve the vacation schedule," then I know we have narrowed the gap.

During negotiations, he explained, he listened to see how often issues were mentioned after the initial meetings, and which were cited frequently and called "very important to the membership." That would be "a clue, and not a very subtle clue, saying you have to pay attention to this area." Another lawyer said, "If the union doesn't talk about an issue every time, you know it's not important to them." And yet another said, "The people I negotiate with know that, when we get to the end, I say 'this is the best offer we'll put on the table.' I suspect the guy knows we're just about there. There are still a few moves left."

It was usually the responsibility of the lead bargainer to know the signals and interpret them for his or her team. After one round of negotiations at the Hartford Centrum, Mike Ross had to explain to his disappointed team that some issues that were ostensibly "rejected" by management were not really rejected. The company, he pointed out, asked some questions about the union's proposals after stating that they were rejected. In this way the company was "signaling" that it was willing to talk about those issues. Ross explained that the job of the company's negotiator was to be "readable" and showed that he was the one who was able to do the reading. Much of the communication, from that time for forward, occurred between the two lead bargainers. As one company lawyer explained, "If there is an experienced negotiator, I target him or her while talking to the whole committee. They will interpret what I am saying just as I will interpret for my client what the union is saying."

As with discounting, signaling only works if there is confidence in the other side's ability to read the signals. At Hartford Ross explained that he could count on Garofano to understand their position because he brought a deck of cards with him during the last days of negotiations. If Garofano knew enough to expect hours of "downtime" during negotiations, Ross could probably count on him to know how to read the union's signals. As one IH company negotiator put it, "[Skilled negotiators] can pretty well evaluate what are the most important issues, which ones will probably go away, which ones can be settled with a minimum of difficulty, and which ones will be the so-called last-minute issues that are strike issues to either side."

But less skilled negotiators were not as adept at signaling. One company lawyer was greatly frustrated by the behavior of a union rep who was new to bargaining, "I found that to be one of the most difficult negotiations because the signals coming across the table did not mean anything; he did not understand the language of negotiation." This rep gave the usual laundry list of proposals but did not signal what the union's priorities were. There was "no way," this lawyer argued, that the company could "intelligently respond to that set of proposals" because it did not know what was "excess baggage and what were the priorities."

He would put things aside and not discuss them at all, and you thought they were dead. Normally when that happens they are gone. With this guy, they weren't gone. When you were starting to get close on the other issues, they would reappear. In trying to fashion the cost of the package, you could not count on anything . . . Here you were on the last day of negotiations and you just had no idea how many issues were still on the table. With him, you never knew.

In another negotiation this lawyer had problems on his own side when the owner he represented was inadvertently sending inaccurate signals:

My client insisted on getting into the negotiations toward the end, and he was transmitting signals across that table. If I had not had a very bright [union negotiator] on the other side, he would have said to himself, "Oh, this is an area where I can get improvements." The guy said to me, "You are better off telling your client not to sit in negotiations or not to speak, because he is sending signals that some of my people are picking up, and I know he does not mean what he is saying."

Private Conversations

An alternative to signaling and discounting is to meet in private, away from the audience, and away from the need to stay in role.

This occurred in nearly all negotiations (although a few negotiators refused to have private meetings, or were barred by constituents for political concerns from doing so).

Private ("sidebar") meetings are important for several reasons. First, in private meetings it is not necessary to maintain a
facade. As one union lawyer put it, "I am not trying to impress
my clients. In that environment, communication is much more
candid."[3] A company lawyer described recent negotiations
where he arranged for both teams to go home, "No committee
members, no management members, let's see if we can settle it.
[In that case,] without all of the posturing and such, we settled in
a half hour." In private, negotiators can say things about their
own team that they cannot say in public and can tell the other
negotiator how to avoid certain political pitfalls, as well as the
best timing to influence a committee. One experienced bargainer
at IH explained:

What you do is continually test, "Is it the right time to make a move," and,
if we do make a move, "What are the hot buttons." You're not going to get
a clear signal that says "Hey, the union's ready to move on mandatory
overtime." What you're going to get is, "Hey, why don't you try this kind
of approach." And it may be nothing more than a way to start the conversation going. Or the message might be, "Why did you present the issue that
way? You really screwed up." Well, how did I screw up? "Well, did you
know that Bill at Louisville feels this way about it and he's got a particular
issue." Sometimes how you present things can either turn them on or turn
them off.

Second, negotiators feel that they may become committed to
an exploratory idea if they state it publicly. Constituents (if they
hear about the idea), team members, or opponents all may
become convinced that an agreement has been made, even if it
was just an idea. That may limit the negotiator's ability later to
create new packages or make better trades. Third, as information

---

3. In experiments conducted by Klimoski and Ash (1974), negotiators had a harder
time arriving at a solution when they felt they had less freedom in their negotiations
due to the existence of an audience.

flows through groups, it can be easily distorted. One union rep said, "If there are ten men in a line, and at one end you say that the sky is red, by the end the sky is blue." For that reason he preferred sidebars.[4] Fourth, sidebar discussions allow negotiators (who often have several negotiations to deal with at once) to manage the logistics of ongoing negotiating. Referring to arbitrations, a union lawyer explained, "A guy will call you a pile of shit in court, but out of court you can deal with him on the side and ask a favor of a two-week delay."

Finally, signaling is an inexact science. Negotiators often want to make sure that people are making the right interpretations. As one company lawyer put it: "Those discussions often prove very helpful because the signals may not be that clear across the table; there may be some misunderstanding." Toward the end of negotiations, especially, is a "time when you really have to have an off-the-record discussion with your counterpart" and make sure that the signals are understood.

Meeting away from the committee is sometimes a delicate issue for the union team. At Hartford, before Ross met with Garofano in private, he was careful to tell his team what he was doing and why, "Sometimes it helps to talk off the record. You don't have to deal with the BS." He went on to explain to them the role of a mediator, who provided the legitimating context for many of the private meetings:

You can say things to a mediator without it crossing to their side; you can float ideas. If you did that across the table, they would beat you down, whereas with a mediator you can tell them where you are. I'm a lot more secure out there with a mediator. If it was Carl Perry negotiating [the lawyer who had previously led negotiations for the company], I'd be a lot

---

4. Mike Ross, at Hartford, made an explicit agreement with his team that he would share information with them only if they kept it to themselves. He explained, "The worst thing that can happen is leaks from the table. I know it is not democratic, and it sounds like Poland, but you can't let everything go out, because say they offered 5%—in 20 minutes that is 25% [in the gossip circles] and if you don't deliver it, everybody is pissed off."

more confident, but this guy [Garofano] is new. When you float ideas [with the mediator], you can make mistakes. You can take it back. In full committee, if you say something and they take it, you think, "Gee, did I make a mistake?"

Explicit Collusion in Producing a Joint Performance

In these cases negotiators depended on their opponents to help them perform well for constituents. You might even say that they colluded in the production of a joint performance. Sometimes the collusion was implicit, when each expected the other to know how to discount, generate signals, and interpret signals. Sometimes it was more explicit.

At the most mundane level negotiators sometimes warned the opponent about particular political problems, timing issues, or performance needs. One union lawyer said that if he knew a company lawyer well, the lawyer would warn him if a particular client "needs to feel that he fought a tough fight." In those cases he knew that they would have to "wait until the last minute" to make an agreement. Another union lawyer heard his union rep tell the opposing management negotiator in private, "I need this [change]—I promised it." He added, "If it is possible, they will give it. For political reasons, they want to help Bob." Management wants the union rep to look good for his or her team.

Sometimes the collusion was more elaborate. At NBP the union team included one negotiator who was being especially stubborn. The lead bargainer and the rest of the union team felt that her intransigence was based on a repeated misunderstanding of the calculations and was interfering with their ability to get a good agreement. Finally, the problem was so bad that they secretly asked the company's lead bargainer to come down hard on her. He did this, she backed away from her position, and productive negotiations resumed.

The final moves that led to mediation at the Hartford Centrum were similarly orchestrated by the lead bargainers. On the fourth day of negotiations, with the deadline two weeks away, Ross told the committee, "I don't see any movement. We're headed for an impasse. I'm gonna go talk with John and say our position hasn't changed. Why don't we go for mediation?" When negotiations resumed, Ross delivered the following statement, with just a hint of anger and annoyance in his voice: "We've read your offer and given it the consideration that it deserves, about three minutes. We're not going to move until you do; you won't until we do. We might as well go to mediators. We've done it the last three times." Garofano responded, "If you think it would help." Later Ross explained to me in greater detail what had happened during an earlier meeting with Garofano. Ross told Garofano that, because of work schedules and member expectations, it was "useless to vote in September." Therefore "someone would get hurt" if the company gave its final offer too early: Either the company would have to pay more than it planned, or the guys would reject the contract, strike, and would get hurt financially. As a result Garafano intentionally stalled the negotiations by presenting a low offer. This helped Ross by justifying a delay in negotiations and making the timing of the negotiations better for ratification. It allowed the committee to look good by bringing the negotiations to the Federal Mediation and Conciliation Service.[5]

In these cases and others, negotiators colluded in their effort to get individual negotiators, the union committee, or constituents to "accept reality" at the appropriate time. The problem

5. The shift to mediation, as Ross saw it, was important not only as a way of reaching a deal but as a way to show that he had brought the negotiations to the last possible step and thus had pushed as hard as possible for his cause. He explained: "Mediation is a waste of time. Maybe you get a few ideas. More important is that it looks good for the committee. They need to be able to say that they tried as hard as possible. They have to come out looking good."

was generated by the practice, prior to negotiations, of building union expectations and solidarity. Raising hopes helped the union gain power, but then the lead bargainer had to "break the committee" when he or she had achieved as much as was realistic. Often the company's lead bargainer would help.

The Benefits of Private Communication

Negotiators have good reasons to share very little information with the opponent and to distort what information is shared. Hiding and distorting information is considered good strategy: Schelling (1960) pointed out that negotiators gain leverage by making the opponent believe that they cannot possibly move from a position. Experimental research (Rubin and Brown 1975, 267) has shown that negotiators can win more by starting with extreme first offers. Maintaining an unswerving public position can help mobilize constituents in case of a strike.[6] In addition distorting information is part of the public drama of negotiations; negotiators are expected to express outrage at the opponent's insensitivity, defend the righteousness of their position, and argue that they will fight to the end to defend a hallowed tradition, even though their position is much more complex.

Despite these reasons to hide and distort information, negotiators actually go to great lengths to privately create clarity and understanding between the two sides. While negotiators may begin with shows of open antagonism, they eventually share information through a gradual process of sending and receiving. Given the risks involved with developing backstage relations with the opponent, why do they do it?

---

6. One union rep explained, "I could not say publicly we would give up [our proposal] for a trade, because, for our posture at the time, we did not want them to realize that we would compromise. If there was a strike, it would be over the issue of health care. We needed to uphold that public position."

The Need for Full Information

Most negotiators feel that sharing information is critical. As one union rep explained, if he "goes to the table with 20 issues, 4 or 5 are necessary—others can be watered down. That *has to be known* halfway through the negotiations." Clarity gets even more important toward the end of negotiations. Another union rep said, "Nobody is honest at the beginning of bargaining. In the last moments, it gets very honest. Decisions count." Even though both sides bluff, distort, and manipulate information, negotiators value communication greatly. A union lawyer explained, "Two things are critical: total unquestioned integrity and attempts to communicate. I'd rather have an employer tell us, 'if you strike, we'll break it. I've got 300 strike breakers.' Anything that interrupts communication is bad, what helps communication is good."

Negotiators want to be able to make their decisions based on relatively full and accurate information (i.e., they want to be in the situation imagined in game theory models of negotiations). It is fine to operate with a great deal of ambiguity early in negotiations, but it is not fine to make critical decisions without an understanding of their real implications. At Hartford Ross did not want to make his final proposal until he knew that it would be acceptable to the company. At HCI Moore based his decisions on a clear sense of where the two sides would meet in their concession pattern. And the company lawyer who complained that his opponent did not signal properly was greatly frustrated by his inability to know what was on the table, calculate where to put the available money, and know how to make his next move. Like the game theorist who needs to simplify the model to have a determinate outcome, negotiators want to face a situation where the outcome is calculable and determinate in their eyes. The simplicity of game theory models does not represent what happens when negotiations begin, but it may well represent the situation that negotiators like to face in the final stages of bargaining.[7]

Of course this is not to say that negotiators are completely open with each other. They are still out to win, they expect distortions, and, as a union lawyer put it, "There is a certain amount of deceit that goes on. We're competitive. We get egotistical. You hate to lose on any one issue." Explained another union rep, "When I lay my cards out, I always keep a few in reserve. I use every advantage I can." Yet overall, negotiators are much more open with each other in private than one might imagine, given the advantages than can be gained by secrecy and distortion and the degree to which they act more cautious in public.

Supporting the Main-Table Performance

Receiving information about the opponent's priorities or political concerns enables negotiators to give a better, more skillful performance. Without accurate information negotiators are likely to make moves that backfire on them. If they stumble badly— unable to accurately predict the opponent's moves or unable to manage the situation—they will not look skilled or in control. To stay in character as lead bargainer requires more information than is typically conveyed in public. Lead bargainers on both sides need each other's help if they are to stay in role. Any attempt by a lead bargainer to break down these private contacts would make it more difficult for them, as well, to deliver a skilled performance. Providing a more skillful performance may

---

7. In the words of decision theorists, negotiators are not absolutely rational, but they are boundedly rational (March and Simon 1958): They want to face situations that, because they are limited and somewhat simplified, allow them to see the options that are available, weigh the costs and benefits of each option, and pick the course of action that maximizes their utility. Given some limits, it is possible for them to feel that they are acting, and indeed act, in a fully rational manner.

help in turn to enhance team confidence in the negotiator so that he or she is allowed more freedom to engage in private talks with the opponent, which, again, can enhance his or her ability to give a skilled performance.[8]

Opponents have good reason to share information with each other, patiently playing the straight man in each other's performance, and even colluding with each other in order to make the performance effective. If they hurt the opponent's ability to perform well and to share information with them, they hurt their own bargaining position. In the end each side's constituent relations is a problem for *both* negotiators, and the performance they give is a joint one.

The Social Basis of Backstage Work

These mechanisms for private, off-stage communication are delicate and risky. Information that is shared in sidebar meetings can be used against negotiators, the very existence of private meetings can be a political risk for them, and the use of signals depends on the opponent's skill in reading and sending them. Backstage work requires a strong social foundation: Lead bargainers have to know each other, be able to depend on their shared knowledge of the rituals of bargaining, and be confident in each other's veracity. Lead bargainers have to fulfill the behavioral expectations of opposing lead bargainers as well as teammates and constituents if they expect to have any private means of communication during negotiations.

---

8. This scenario is similar to Adams's (1976) classic analysis of "boundary spanners." According to Adams, constituent monitoring decreases when the boundary spanner delivers good results to constituents. Decreased monitoring then allows the boundary spanner to work more closely with opponents, which produces more influence over them and thus better deals for constituents and, once again, more freedom to work closely with opponents. In my scenario what matters in this cycle is not just delivering the goods but delivering the act—producing a skilled performance that convinces observers that the negotiator is loyal, leaderlike, and energetic. Negotiators have to deliver some of the goods, but, just as important, they have to show that they got the goods in the right way.

At a minimum negotiators expect of their opposites consistency and stability in their actions. That allows negotiators to predict future behavior based on the past—in other words, to know the opponent's habits or tendencies. Negotiators can build up some expectations as a result of their familiarity with their opponents. At HCI, for example, Moore explained:

> It is critical to remind yourself who you are dealing with. If you deal with the same people, recall how they reacted to the same situation: Do they feel the need to be belligerent for show at the beginning? Do they meet off the record before negotiations? Remind yourself that with this union they hold out until the last hour. See if they are a union that likes to trade.

During interviews, negotiators were able to describe, in some detail, the habits and tendencies of each of the people they had worked with. One union rep described his management counterpart: "He knows me, I know him. Whatever he can extract from the company, he puts on the table as a final proposal." And a union lawyer explained that she expected one particular company lawyer to be overly legalistic, so she had to work around him to make a deal. Whatever these negotiators thought of their opponent's particular style, at least they knew what to expect. Negotiators want to be familiar with the other person because "the more you know about a person, you're more apt to read the person accurately."

Beyond just knowing a person's habits, negotiators expect their opponent to be familiar with the process. If the opponent is a skilled bargaining "pro," then the negotiator can count on the opponent to negotiate in the way that is expected, and know at least the basics of interpreting, signaling, and managing political pressures.[9] If the opponents are new to bargaining, their actions

---

9. Skilled negotiators will also know how to keep their signals simple and clear. If cooperation is to be maintained through a process of reciprocity (e.g., the "tit-for-tat" rule for iterated prisoner's dilemma games), it is important that each party's moves be simple and clearly interpretable; the system breaks down if one side tries to be too "clever" (Axelrod 1984, 120).

might be taken without an understanding of their implications. It is easier to depend on one's expectations if the other knows the system. As Gambetta (1988) put it, even in a competition, we need to be able to trust that the other knows the rules.

Negotiators also expect their opponents' overt statements to be accurate and their promises to be fulfilled. One union lawyer explained: "They have to trust you. If you lie one time, there will be no end to the problems." A company lawyer made a similar point, "I don't like to be in a position of defending a lot of things that I'm prepared to concede. I hurt my credibility by doing that. They don't believe you if you say 'no, no, no,' then suddenly back down." Another company lawyer explained that it was critical for the opponent to understand that "you are going to be honest across that table and you are not going to try to mislead them."

Finally, negotiators hope that their opponents will abide by the spirit of an agreement and be fair when new, unforeseen issues develop. A union rep described a particular CEO: "If he says that this is what we agreed on, I'd sign it tomorrow. If I have a question about a clause, I can call him and he'll fix it. He has integrity." The opposite of integrity is meanness—going the extra mile to hurt the opponent. One union lawyer described a company lawyer: "I just don't trust him. I know in the end that [other lawyers] would never screw me or embarrass me. But [this lawyer] would come back at me later and let the union know 'we screwed you.'"

In sum, negotiators expect of their opponents stability of character, skill, credibility, and integrity. Underlying all of these expectations is trust. At the most basic level negotiators want to trust that their predicitons for how others will act will turn out to be accurate. This sense of trust is, as Luhmann (1989) put it, "confidence in one's expectations," or as Sitkin and Roth (1991) put it, "an expectation that exchanges or interactions will contin-

ue to be reliable within a particular context."[10] Beyond predictability, negotiators want to trust that the other lead bargainer
will not intentionally hurt them. Lorenz (1992) defines an action
based on this type of trust as one that "(1) increases vulnerability
to another whose behavior is not under one's control, and (2)
takes place in a situation where the future penalty suffered if the
trust is abused would lead one to regret the action" (p. 456). Both
aspects of trust—predictibility and goodwill—help reduce complexity for negotiators and make it possible for them to count on
the opponent in important ways.[11]

Stability of character, skill, credibility, and integrity—and the
trust they make possible—are essential for backstage communications between lead bargainers (see figure 5.2). To know how to
interpret the actions of an opponent, it is critical to know the
opponent's character and tendencies. Moore, drawing on his
experience with the union, judged its tough stance on medical
coverage to be a ploy, "I just know that they hold out until the
end. That's their history. I just went over my '86 notes," he
explained to his teammate. Similarly at Hartford Ross worried
that his interpretation of Garofano's actions might be inaccurate
because he had never negotiated with Garofano before.
Negotiators' ability to interpret the opponent's actions depends
on familiarity and trust in the stability of their character.

To *signal* the opponent, a negotiator must know that the opponent is not only familiar with him or her but skilled enough to
competently interpret the signals that are sent. In the HCI case

---

10. This aspect of trust is similar to Garfinkel's (1967) notion of background expectations: It governs all of the minute details of how people interact and is often not recognized until a violation occurs.
11. As Luhmann (1979) put it, a system built on trust is more "rational" than one
that is not: "It is precisely this differentiation of the approaches to trust and distrust
which is, from the point of view of the system, rational. For it assists it in preserving
the higher level of inner order in comparison to its environment; or, in other words,
is stabilizing, in an extremely complex environment, a simpler, less-complex sys-
tem-order which is suited to human capacities for action" (p. 91).

Moore explained (prior to bargaining) that he had to make sure that the union was familiar with his style and signals and would even ask the mediator to inform the union of that if needed. For example, the union had to know what he meant by "best offer" versus "final offer." And, at Hartford, Ross was relieved when he saw evidence that Garofano was a "pro"—Ross could then count on him to follow his moves. Signaling depends on trust in the opponents' skills, in addition to their stability of character.

Finally, to hold *sidebar* discussions (or engage in joint performances), negotiators must not only be familiar with the opponents and be confident in their negotiating skill but also be able to count on their credibility and integrity.[12] In side meetings negotiators can be quite vulnerable: Information is exchanged that cannot be checked out easily because it is off the record or because it is being used too quickly to verify. In these ways predictability and trust allow lead bargainers to convey information so that each can make better calculations about the negotiations, avoid costly mistakes, and perform better for their constituents and teammates.

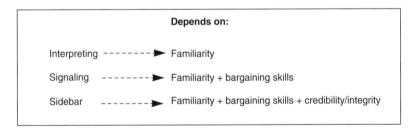

Figure 5.2
The social basis of backstage strategies

---

12. Pruitt (1971) argued that "negotiators will engage in informal conferences only to the extent that they trust their opponent to adhere to" a set of norms that include the following: "the conference should be kept secret," negotiators should "speak truthfully" about their flexibilities, and "agreements reached in informal conferences should be honored when the formal meetings reconvene" (p. 225).

Credibility and integrity provide an additional benefit as well. They make it possible for lead bargainers to make deals based on personal promises, handshakes, and goodwill. Where there is confidence in the veracity of the opposing bargainer, deals are easier to make, since all possible contingencies do not have to be spelled out in advance.[13] At HCI, after much wrangling over how to write contract language specifying order of layoff, the union's lead bargainer accepted his opponent's word on the matter: "It's hard to write it out. I'd accept from you, Jeff, to just say that the janitor will be the first out the door."[14] By contrast, when there is no trust, coming to agreement is more difficult. A company lawyer said that there were some union negotiators "who I would not settle a matter with unless I had something in writing. I would be afraid there might be a misinterpretation of what we arrived at." Where there is no relationship between the lead bargainers, a union lawyer pointed out, negotiations are more "protracted, venomous, and frustrating."

Judging Opponent Trustworthiness

Given the importance of trust, lead bargainers monitor each other very carefully to gather information about the opponent's tendencies, credibility, and integrity. One company lawyer

---

13. These types of informal agreements are called "relational" contracts in legal circles (Goetz and Scott 1981). In many situations it is impossible to write out all contingencies in a contract or to foresee what contingencies might develop. As a result many contracts include broad clauses about "best efforts," and many business deals bypass contracts altogether, depending on a handshake instead (Macaulay 1963). This type of contracting is especially prevalent in Japan, where relationships are highly stable and *not* "affectively neutral." As a result, argues Dore (1983), people can plan "without bitchiness" and tend to make more investments. He calls this "X efficiency" and claims that it helps the Japanese outperform the United States economically.
14. The kind of deal that Moore and Hutchinson made at HCI is not unusual. As a union lawyer put it, "Much of the business is a handshake. When you negotiate at 4 AM and ask for closure, the guy says, 'You don't need it—you've got my word.'"

explained that he expected a new union negotiator who represented a bargaining unit to check him out: "I know he called the
lawyer that represents his union to find out what he can about
me." If negotiators believe they have a good reputation, they
encourage such checking. "When I met with this guy, I dropped
a few names of union agents in Rhode Island so he could check
me out. I have a good reputation." Reputation is something that
negotiators depend on and go to great lengths to protect. One
negotiator explained: "You cannot afford to allow anybody to
attack your integrity without a defense and without their understanding that you value your integrity."

A more salient source of knowledge about negotiators is
direct personal experience.[15] A company lawyer described building a relationship with his opponent: "We spent a lot of time
together. We confided some things to him and we gained his
confidence. He had no reason to question our sincerity." As
negotiators come to know each other, what is most important is
past actions. As one blunt union rep described a lawyer who had
failed to deliver what he said, "The lawyer tried to trick me. He
is a sleaze." Negotiators do not easily forget any instances of
meanness or breaches of trust.

Negotiators also look for signs of professionalism.[16] One company negotiator worried about "brand new" union business
agents, but otherwise felt confident that "business agents on the
whole . . . know what the process is and they go to school for it."
One union negotiator could not be trusted because, according to

---

15. Negotiators are so attentive to information about their opponents' character that
even training sessions become a context ripe with implications for the relationship
between opponents. After a day of joint training at Texas Bell, a union negotiator
explained that management's behavior during the simulations was thought to represent their tendencies in real negotiations: "You learn who is a gambler, and who is
not—who will be honest, and who will run chances to lose it all." "[It helps to] see
people in different positions on different issues," added another union leader.
16. Pruitt (1971) recognized that although the most important element of developing
trust with the opponent is experience, "to some extent recognition that he is a sea-
soned professional can substitute for such experience" (p. 225).

a company lawyer, "He is too ideological—he doesn't believe in the effects of competition." If a negotiator is a professional, it is to safe to assume that he or she accepts the basic tenets of the labor relations system, including the right of workers to be represented by a union and the right of managers to manage, and knows the rituals of bargaining.

Finally, negotiators make their judgments to some degree based on personal chemistry. According to a union rep, "The integrity of the negotiator is formed in the first meeting. If you know each other from before, it is carried on. If he is new, you make your judgments early on." Even for those who have frequent contact, it is not just past actions that generate trust but strong affective bonds.[17] One company lawyer said about a particular union lawyer, "That is a guy I would trust implicitly. We will not bullshit each other. . . . [He] and I have a very close relationship."

In these ways negotiators watch each other and know that they are being watched. They look for behaviors that meet expectations of professionalism and integrity, and adjust their use of backstage strategies to match the opponents's apparent level of trustworthiness. Since these expectations are held by many (if not most) labor negotiators, the behaviors that they reward have developed into norms within the collective bargaining community, and a culture exists that places a high value on integrity and professionalism.[18] Most negotiators know that their work will me made much easier if they abide by these expectations; they will be given more information, treated with greater

---

17. This type of trust is close to what Zucker (1986) calls "character" trust. She emphasizes that character trust occurs based on judgments of the other's background, such as family or gender. She calls the kind of trust that is based on observing past actions, such as those discussed above, "process" trust.

18. Elswhere (Friedman 1992b) I have called this subculture the "culture of mediation." The term refers to norms of behavior and values held by those in interstitial positions between groups, such as negotiators, that serve the function of translating, conveying, and receiving meaning across groups in conflict.

respect, and not be subject to retaliatory actions by the opposing lead bargainer.

Negotiators' judgments about each other are especially influential when they anticipate doing business in the future.[19] As one union leader explained, "An ongoing relationaship is best—you can't screw each other. You work together constantly. So you always have a threat." As a union lawyer put it:

It is important professionally for me to maintain my relationship with my adversaries. One's close friends are on the other side. I see *them*, not other labor lawyers. It doesn't do you any good to destroy any one of them in any given case. It comes back to you.

In some situations the future contact is another negotiation. Among labor lawyers in a small community, for example, most negotiators know each other and can expect to meet in the future. One lawyer explained that, in his city, "You don't see that many new faces. You don't see lawyers who don't do labor work, doing labor work." In other situations the future contact is the ongoing work that union leaders and labor relations managers do between contracts. One labor leader explained that his opponents in negotiations were "folks that we deal with on an everyday basis, personnel directors, vice presidents for human resources, people that we know and have established a relationship with." Even when negotiators may not encounter each

---

19. Axelrod (1984) says that "as long as the interaction is not iterated, cooperation is very difficult. That is why an important way to promote cooperation is to arrange that the same two individuals will meet each other again" (p. 125). In one striking example, he tells the story of World War I soldiers sitting opposite each other in trenches for long periods of time. They learned not to attack each other, knowing that to do so would just result in an enemy attack on them. As long as the same people faced each other across the battlefield, an implicit agreement developed not to disturb each other. This was a great source of frustration for generals on both sides. One might argue that the existence of sanctions of this type means that we are no longer talking about trust. I would disagree. The ability to sanction someone in the future may make a negotiator more confident that the opponent will not act inappropriately, but the opponent can take actions that would cause great damage in the current situation and, as Lorenz put it, lead the negotiator to regret his or her trusting behaviors.

other again directly, knowing that one's reputation may affect negotiations with others produces, as Axelrod (1984) put it, a "shadow of the future." Wherever there is a dense network of either direct or indirect contacts, lead bargainers can be more confident in their ability to trust each other.

Therefore negotiator judgments about their opponents are based not only on personal observations but on structural factors as well, such as the existence of a collective bargaining community and the likelihood of direct contacts in the future. Where there is a well-connected community, negotiators can make their judgments much more confidently, and they can depend on the community to make judgments for them. Where there is ongoing direct contact with the opponent, negotiators have more information about the opponent, and more opportunities for recourse if their judgment is wrong. As one union rep put it, "The key to good, productive labor relations in my eyes is not only the consistency of answers to problems, but also that the people who make those decisions are in there as long as possible. The relationship between the parties is more important than the written contract."

Front Stage and Backstage

While the front stage of negotiations is filled with rituals of opposition, representation, and control, backstage negotiators communicate with each other more freely and without much of the rancor that is expressed in public. While conflict is expressed in public, understanding is built up in private. It is here that more of the integrative aspects of negotiations take place. The particular strategies that are used to create backstage interactions are well known in the negotiation literature; what has been missed is the ways in which these strategies require a strong social foundation. They depend on negotiators' ability to accurately predict how the process will unfold and to have faith in the credibility and integrity of the opposing lead bargainer. They depend on the existence of a highly connected community of bargainers that reinforces the values of stability, predictability, and trust.

6   The Logic and Limits of the Traditional Process

The Social Logic of Traditional Bargaining Rituals

Over the last four chapters the traditional negotiation process was explained in terms of the strategic *and* social dynamics of labor negotiations. While most bargaining theories focus exclusively on the strategic moves that make sense for two parties facing each other across the bargaining table, this analysis also incorporates the issues that negotiators face when bargaining is done in groups. The existence of groups adds three levels of complexity. First, accomplishing any strategic plan requires that group processes and social impressions be properly managed: Control depends on group cohesion and the acceptance of the influence of group leaders. Second, certain behaviors may be required to satisfy observers, regardless of whether they are ones that are most useful for strategic purposes: Constituents and teammates expect negotiators to act in ways that reassure them of their loyalty and dedication to the cause. Third, negotiators' actions may be oriented to interpersonal goals such as acceptance as a team member or leader that have inherent benefits for them as individuals in addition to their instrumental benefits for negotiations.

Underlying all of these challenges is the need for negotiators to enact the social structure of negotiations and establish their place in it; they are continuously defining for themselves and others what the relevant groups are in negotiations and what their relationship is with these groups. The basic structure is given: There are two sides, with constituents and representatives on each side, and leaders within each team. The problem is to make the categories of opponent, representative, and leader socially real, fulfill the behavioral expectations associated with these roles, and convince others that you are who you claim to be. Negotiators expend great effort conveying an idealized version of themselves and their group to teammates, constituents, and opponents.

Managerial negotiators show themselves as defenders of economic rationality and opponents of union interference with managerial discretion and free-market exchange. Union negotiators show themselves as opponents of managerial greed and defenders of worker rights and fair wages. Each displays their opposition to the other side, and common bonds with each other. As representatives, negotiators show not only their agreement with group goals but their willingness to be dogged and determined in pursuit of their goals; they listen carefully to constituent concerns, present them with vigor to the other side, and fight as long and hard as possible to achieve constituents' goals. And lead bargainers show not only that they are of their group and determined to pursue their goals but also that they are skilled, experienced, and in control. In as much as the traditional process expresses an idealized version of the social order, it is not just an expression of rational strategic calculation but also a ritual that carries meaning.

Throughout this process negotiators both control and are controlled by those who watch them; these observers have expectations for how negotiators should act, and negotiators act in order to shape their perceptions and actions. On a broader level the social structure of negotiations defines a set of roles and behaviors for negotiators, but that social structure is reproduced only when negotiators enact it through their public performances. The social structure of bargaining exists in the interplay between audience expectations and negotiator actions.

It is these social dynamics that motivate many of the behaviors that are observed in traditional negotiations. The traditional process is stable because the public rituals that are so common to it—displays of opposition, representation, and control—help negotiators to achieve their personal and strategic goals and to manage the many political pressures that they face. The system also survives because it provides mechanisms for learning and adaptation. Lead bargainers are able to use the public rituals to gradually sharpen and focus their goals (especially on the union side), and they are able to use backstage strategies to communicate more with the opponent than is allowed in public. As long as lead bargainers have confidence in the predictability and integrity of their opposite, they are able to both orchestrate public rituals of conflict and engage in private rituals of trust and communication.

Returning to Walton and McKersie

The model presented here has many of the same elements as Walton and McKersie's behavioral theory of negotiations, but it adds some clarification about the relationship between the elements of their model. Integrative and distributive bargaining are both part of negotiations, but they are done on different stages; the public drama of negotiations is distributive, while much of the integrative process occurs in private. One of the key skills of the lead bargainer is knowing how to perform differently in

these settings, and how to manage the shift between the different stages. Attitudinal restructuring is also seen in this model,
but it has a specific role to play in the process. It occurs predominantly between lead bargainers and, when it works, is used to
enhance their ability to engage in integrative bargaining in private even though distributive tactics are being played out in
public. And, most important, central to both integrative and distributive tactics is the management of intraorganizational
dynamics, including not just internal bargaining but also the
many ways in which people try to gain influence and acceptance
in the group. The traditional system is not just made up of four
parts; it constitutes an integrated whole that is held together by
public displays and careful management of impressions.

Nonlabor Applications

Though the approach presented here was developed through
observations of labor negotiations, it is applicable to other negotiating contexts as well. The distinctive feature that makes this
approach relevant is that the negotiations are done by groups
and some degree of observation and political pressure is felt by
at least one of the parties. One example of a similar situation is
international negotiations.

In international negotiations, as with labor negotiations, "the
unitary actor assumption is often radically misleading" (Putnam
1988, 433): Top negotiators are not always unified and negotiators face complex trade-offs among different domestic groups
(Druckman 1978). As a result negotiations are characterized by a
mixture of public facade and private understandings. In one
example, Putnam describes the way in which German politicians
reacted to proposals for worldwide economic stimulus at the
Bonn summit of 1978: For domestic political purposes they put
on public displays of opposition, while privately supporting the

plan. As Zartman and Berman (1982) put it, international negoti-ations "involve a good deal of intragroup, interagency, home-to-mission, actor-to-audience negotiations" (p. 207). With the need to keep up a public facade, international negotiators use a great deal of signaling and "behind the scenes talks" for communica-tion (Zartman and Berman, p. 177). Ikle (1964) describes how international negotiators often meet secretly to avoid constituent pressures, or bargain informally to be freed from the expected (and, in his eyes, highly inefficient) rituals of formal negotia-tions. In one example, Zartman and Berman describe how "Russians and Americans paired off after hours during the SALT talks to get their message across better than they could in ple-nary session"(p. 210), and they point out the growing tension between private communication and negotiating in groups:

Each side in a negotiation is expected to speak with one voice, and yet a delegation usually has more than one member. Before diplomacy became a bureaucratic function the negotiator was often on his own, attended at most by a personal aide. Today, negotiating teams can—and often must—be enormous because of the technical complexity of the issues, although real movement still is often accomplished by a few chief negotiators meet-ing together. At the Geneva conference on the Middle East, in late 1973, Foreign Ministers Gromyko and Eban were in a room with three Russian and three Israeli aides when Gromyko said, "Look, something strange is occurring. Sitting here are six men who are thinking the same thing: 'How can we leave our two ministers so they can speak alone?'" The six aides got the hint and left. (p. 206)

Group dynamics, leadership, and trust between opponents also play a role in international negotiations. When negotiators do meet with their teams, according to Zartman and Berman, it is critical that someone on each team be able to lead the group and that group members learn to understand and accept each other. They quote Averall Harriman as saying, "the morale of the team is extremely important, and the chairman of the group has to be a fellow who can pull people together" (p. 215). And Ikle (1964) argues that familiarity and trust between lead bargainers helps ensure that each side understands the other's positions:

Intimate acquaintance with a diplomat helps to assess his thoughts and motives. To put it crudely: friendship is a source of intelligence. In public as in private affairs, there is that intuitive understanding of a man which may reveal how strongly he means what he says and what his basic intentions are. Whereas a close personal relation between diplomats need not lead to greater frankness, it makes dissimulation more difficult. Between diplomats of friendly countries, it may strengthen reciprocal trust; and between hostile nations, it may at least make communication more meaningful for both sides. (p. 160)

There is no existing study of international negotiation that reproduces in full the arguments developed in this book, but there are many indications in the existing literature that the dynamics I have described are present in international negotiations as well as labor negotiations. The theory may be applicable to other contexts as well. Community negotiations over issues such as waste disposal, public investments, and environmental laws are also filled with public performances, since they are highly watched and politicized (Susskind and Cruikshank 1987; Gray 1989). And negotiators in many types of bargaining have to play out roles as representatives, opponents, and leaders. As long as negotiations involve groups rather than individuals on each side, they must manage social processes—both because bargaining strategies depend on them and because they are an inherent part of any meeting of people in groups.

Flaws in the Traditional System

In many ways the system of public conflict and backstage communication constitutes a reasonable response to the social demands placed on negotiators and is highly functional: It helps negotiators maintain an idealized image of themselves, their team, and their community, it helps them to meet the behavioral expectations that are associated with the negotiator role, and it helps them to achieve control over information and impressions that help them to carry out a bargaining strategy. At the same time in the previous chapters we have seen indications that the process has many risks and flaws. The front-stage drama can heighten conflict and raise expectations beyond what is realistic, and the backstage means of communication are inherently limited. There is much room for valid criticisms of the traditional process.

The Limits of Backstage Work

Backstage interactions between lead bargainers provide some balance to the constrained interactions of the front-stage drama, but depending on the backstage as a way to communicate leaves much at risk. Signals may be misunderstood, sidebar meetings may be restricted, and the contributions of nonlead bargainers may be lost.

Oversignaling

Signals convey so much that negotiators worry a great deal about giving inadvertent signals. An action as innocuous as nodding one's head to acknowledge hearing the opponent's comments can cause great worry. During simulated negotiations at Texas Bell (part of training prior to the actual negotiations), one union negotiator became concerned that his nodding would be misread as a signal of agreement. Therefore he stepped out of role to clarify his intentions: "I caught myself nodding as you were talking. Nodding just means I'm hearing what you're saying." The next day, a management negotiator became frustrated when the union read his head-nodding as agreement. He responded with an air of sarcasm and incredulity, "I'll try not to move my head." These negotiators were so sensitive to signaling that they had either to explicitly discuss the meaning of how they moved their bodies or to completely inhibit any physical expressions.

One of the most persistent and constraining rules of signaling is that merely to discuss a proposal means that you are seriously considering it. One manager at Texas Bell who was new to negotiations had just learned this rule, "I heard that it is a norm in bargaining that if you bring up an idea, it is at least semi-serious." And an experienced negotiator explained, "In regular negotiations, you have a signal-sending routine. If the union brings up something, and I talk about it, they will think I'm nibbling at it." Because of the signaling rules, negotiators cannot explore new or creative ideas during negotiations.

Problems Reading Signals

Experienced negotiators become skilled at reading opponents' signals, but still they make mistakes and, at times, feel confused about the meaning of opponents' actions. Indeed it is sometimes unclear when an action is a signal meant to be interpreted, when an action has no intended meaning, and when an action is intended to hide information.

At Western Technologies there were days when management was confused and stymied because it could not figure out what the union meant to convey by its actions. Seven days into negotiations, the company's lead bargainer, Tom Burger, made a proposal on absentee days that he thought might benefit the union and clarify the company's concerns. To his surprise, the union's lead bargainer, Steve Hayes, gave no direct response but indicated that he was "not going to say no or say yes." Rather, he thought it was time for the company to "hear the pain of the committee." He went on to discuss several unrelated grievances. After negotiations, Burger expressed great frustration with the union, "I don't know what message he's giving me. I was pointing out areas I'm interested in, and that's important information, but he cut me off." In the company's caucus meeting, Burger paced restlessly. He had planned all of his moves and counter-moves around the union's response to his signal, so without a union reaction, he had nothing to do. He and other managers became angry at the union negotiators for being so unrespon-sive. The reason for the union's lack of response according to the mediator (but one that was not conveyed to Burger) was that Hayes could not take any actions while the local chairman was absent to deal with a personal emergency. Here signals were not clear, actions were not understood, and the negotiations suffered as a result.

The comments made at Hartford during a union caucus meet-ing show the struggle to understand opponent signals. After the company had rejected a proposal that the union felt was so innocuous that management should have readily accepted it, one union member pondered, "I wonder what he was thinking when he rejected it?" The lead bargainer looked for a deeper sig-nal, "I wonder *what* he was rejecting." Such basic information as why the company rejected a proposal was left for the union team to figure out for itself. And earlier in these negotiations, when one manager moved to a seat at the end of the table, union nego-tiators concluded that he would not be in charge of the negotia-tions. They were wrong. Negotiators often interpret signals correctly, but they are sometimes unable to interpret opponents' behavior, or they arrive at inaccurate interpretations.

The Limits of Sidebar Meetings

Sidebar discussions are much clearer ways to communicate information, but at time negotiators are restricted from meeting away from the table with the opponent. If constituents are very anxious that negotiators might be "selling out," strong pressures are placed on them to contact the opponent only in public. This is a problem that union negotiators are more likely to face:

Union members have less direct authority over the negotiators than managers do, goals are more ambiguous on the union side, trade-offs between different factions are more clearly apparent, and management is more likely to have resources to entice any individual union bargainer than the union has to entice any individual management bargainer. If the lead bargainer does not have an established reputation with the union, or if members were dissatisfied with deals made the last time, the union team may not want to let the bargainer meet privately with the other side. Even when they do meet, how private it really is varies a great deal. Sayles and Strauss (1953) report that local union officials follow a "principle of twos" when they meet with management. They always bring along another person to the meeting in order to avoid suspicion of a deal or a payoff. How much they say in sidebar meetings also varies a great deal. At Texas Bell the union's lead bargainer told his teammates that he trusted his management counterpart and never found him to lie. "He does what he says. But," he added, "he just doesn't tell me much."

Overdependence on Experience and Trust

If both sides have experience bargaining and experience with each other, they are more likely to find backstage ways to communicate. Conversely, dealing with novice negotiators or new relationships can be difficult: If negotiators do not know what is typical in negotiations, they are more likely to misread the opponent's intentions; if lead bargainers do not know and trust each other, they cannot depend on the opponent to read their signals accurately, will not be as comfortable meeting privately, and will not be as likely to believe what they are told in private. At Hartford Mike Ross worried about his ability to count on his new opponent until he confirmed that Garofano was an experienced bargaining pro, and management at Western Technologies went through much handwringing when they learned that a new international rep was assigned to lead the negotiations. Backstage communication can work only if there are bargainers who know the rituals of bargaining and who know each other. When there is frequent turnover in personnel,[1] it is hard to maintain the kind of continuity that builds familiarity and trust.

Risks of the Front-Stage Drama

If the front-stage drama of conflict has an overly strong impact, it can result in outcomes that are dysfunctional for negotiations. If the public drama sets up a high level of conflict between the two sides, reasonable compromise may be difficult and sour relations will linger after negotiations. Several negotiators whom I interviewed told of strikes that occurred because they had to release the emotions that had built up prior to negotiations. When negotiators build unity by raising expectations, promising solutions to complex problems, and portraying the other side as innately bad or lazy, their later actions may be constrained beyond what is strategically useful.

During negotiations, as well, the need to act tough can discourage cooperation from the other side's members, embarrass them so that they cannot compromise, and set off a cycle of uncontrollable conflict. (This is the classic pattern of conflict escalation described by Pruitt and Rubin 1986.) And the need to

---

1. At General Motors managers in several plants tried to shift labor relations away from extensive formal contracts and toward informal arrangements that were more practical and flexible. A typical concern of union officials (based on conversations with GM managers and union officials attending their joint Paid Education Leave training program) is that plant managers are usually promoted after a few years— these union leaders might trust their current manager and be willing to make informal agreements with him or her, but they cannot be sure that any new manager would honor those agreements or even know about them. The tendency for change of personnel to lead to rule making and greater bureaucracy was a phenomenon identified by Gouldner (1952). He argued that new managers, lacking the informal obligations and personal ties of past managers, tend to resort to the use of formal rules in order to have influence over people.

look tough can lead some negotiators to focus their actions primarily on establishing their reputations rather than making a deal. Several labor leaders, for example, thought that the strike at Caterpillar in 1983 was largely due to the fact that these were the first big negotiations for the union's lead bargainer—he had to establish his credentials by taking the workers out on strike.

Another problem with the front-stage rituals is that with so much controlled by the lead bargainer and so little open to discussion, most negotiators are not involved. This isolation causes some to be bored and resentful, and it denies both parties the benefits of their added knowledge and creativity. An example shows what can be lost in the process: At Brick Industries the union was adamant that the machine operators get their break at the same time each day, even though some flexibility would enable the company to keep the machines running constantly. The international union rep argued, almost pro forma, that workers did not want managers to control their break times. At that point a manager who was not the lead bargainer asked one union steward, sitting quietly to the side at the time, why he was not willing to let the break time shift a few minutes earlier or later to meet the company's needs. He responded that if the workers wanted a drink, they had to get it then; the lunch truck came by only once in the morning. The manager asked about the soda machine; the steward said it was empty half the month. When the manager then asked the foreman if that was true, he replied that it was, and he did not have enough money in the till to keep the machine stocked all the time. If the lead bargainers had kept tight control over the discussion, they might not have discovered the simple cause of this problem. When lead bargainers tightly control negotiations, others tend, in caucuses as well as at the main table, to not listen, not contribute, and not care about the negotiations.

While sidebar communication is helpful, most of what the two sides say in public is not informative—they do not reveal real needs and interests. The fact that they make proposals for show only, without a sense of purpose or logic, has caused some to be cynical about the whole process. One management negotiator at Brick Industries, for example, reacted caustically to the union's suggestion that the contract be for 20 months, "Is that where the dart hit the board?" he asked. The union's lead bargainer responded, "It's negotiations. We listed our preference—you can propose what you want." There was little faith in the veracity of each side's claims. To the degree that negotiators are not able, across the table, to develop common understandings of problems, their ability to create solutions for real or complex issues is greatly limited.

The Costs of Ambiguity

Since negotiators cannot say exactly what they are thinking, it is possible for them to assume that they each know what is going on, when really that is not true. At the Lowell negotiations the two sides were at loggerheads over wage issues. They were far apart on their offers but accidentally learned one day that some of their difficulty was due to a misunderstanding about the calculations. The union had intended a particular wage increase proposal to apply only to lower-tiered workers and calculated the cost of its plan based on that. Management applied the increases to all workers and thus thought the union's plan was impossibly costly. Finally finding this difference in calculations did not lead to an immediate agreement, but it showed that the two sides had been unnecessarily frustrated with each other during the previous discussions.

What Exactly Was Our Deal?

Ambiguity had more lasting repercussions in several other cases. At both Texas Bell and Western Technologies the two parties found out that they had left the previous round of negotiations with fundamentally different ideas of their agreements on key issues.

At Western Technologies negotiators had agreed to lump-sum payments instead of wage increases. The union was disappointed by this, but management convinced it that the company could not afford base wage increases for its employees. What the union understood, but what was not explicitly stated, was that the company could not afford base wage increases for anyone. Within a year, however, the company gave wage increases to its engineers and some managers. This infuriated the union and put it at risk politically. The company negotiators, in joint briefings three years later, claimed that they never told the union they would not give managers raises, and in any case, the market for engineers had become unexpectedly tight so they had to give raises. What was actually said in negotiations will never be known. But it is not surprising that in a system where the conversations are ritualized, truncated, and based on signaling, misunderstandings can occur that have negative consequences for the relationship and for future negotiations.

In 1989 at Texas Bell tensions between the two sides were high because of differences over what had been promised in the last negotiations. One veteran union negotiator explained to a new company negotiator, "I walked out of the room in '86 thinking one thing, then we had a different outcome later. At first I thought it was lies. Now, years later, I think it was misperceptions and misunderstanding." Another new company bargainer, feeling tainted by others' mistakes, asked, "Whose responsibility is it to clear up the misunderstandings? I don't want to be thought of as a dishonorable man."

In these two cases the companies were trying to make nonincremental changes. This may have been a major factor contributing to the confusion that resulted from traditional bargaining processes. At Western Technologies they were negotiating over a new idea—lump-sum payments. Neither side anticipated some issues associated with this form of payment, such as whether a worker who retires before the payment date gets a pro-rated portion of the payment. Changes of this sort require extensive discussions across the table; hints and signals are not likely to uncover potentially important issues.

Vulnerability of the Union

Both labor and management negotiators face pressures to fulfill the expectations associated with their roles, but throughout the previous chapters we have seen that the challenges faced by union negotiators are greater than those faced by management negotiators. While both labor and management engage in rituals of opposition, the union depends on these rituals more since their leverage comes from member mobilization, and their very existence is justified in terms of their opposition to management. While both labor and management negotiators have to display their loyalty to constituents, management does not need to monitor their negotiators as much as union members do, since they have more direct access to their negotiators and formal authority over them. Control is easier when there is a small group of people who make final decisions than when negotiator directives come from a political organization made up of highly dispersed and diverse members. And while both labor and management lead bargainers gain control through displays of expertise, union negotiators often have only those displays to rely on when vying for control. In all of these ways the fact that the union is a political organization makes negotiations more difficult, places on them greater performance pressures, and provides them with less room to maneuver.

The fact that the union is a political organization also places greater pressures on their negotiators to lead. With final authority in the hands of a diverse membership, labor negotiators—especially lead bargainers—have to actively manage the process of group learning and internal compromise. It is up to them to create for their side a clear sense of what they really need from the negotiations, and this must be done throughout the negotiation process. The tension between representing and leading is especially strong for union negotiators.

To the degree that the traditional process helps negotiators manage these pressures, it has been especially helpful to union negotiators. At the same time, to the degree that the political structure of unions places especially strong role expectations on their negotiators, those negotiators are less able to adapt quickly to shifts in power relations between the two parties and the pressures for nonincremental change that come with those shifts. With management more willing to hire replacement workers when strikes occur or move operations to nonunion areas, the traditional strategy of tying one's hands may no longer be wise. And, with management bringing more demands to the table themselves and ones that require radical shifts in employee expectations, the traditional process of gradually shaping member demands during negotiations may no longer work. In today's economic and political environment union negotiators may be especially hurt by social constraints that limit the development of alternative bargaining strategies and alternative processes for negotiating.

Current Pressures

Current economic and political pressures have made the weaknesses of the traditional system more apparent than ever before.

As companies face greater competition from abroad, they are cutting jobs at both the managerial and nonmanagerial level. They are being forced to do more with fewer workers, which has required radical changes in how managers do their jobs, how work is organized, and how production processes are established. Thousands of companies have restructured themselves around quality teams or "reengineered" how they do their work. Those employees who have survived the massive layoffs of the 1980s are expected to work smarter and more efficiently, be more flexible, and be more committed to the company and its customers. Economic pressures have also created new challenges in areas such as health care, where innovative solutions are needed if customary benefits are to be provided for employees in the future. Any diminution of creativity in bargaining or enhancement of adversarialism is now more likely to have an impact on businesses' ability to survive. Economic pressures have led to straightforward requests for union concessions and give-backs, for sure, but they have also made it necessary for labor and management to find solutions to increasingly complex problems across the bargaining table, using fewer resources and causing as little damage to the labor-management relationship as possible.

In the face of these economic pressures, it is management that is taking the lead to create change. As Kochan, Katz, and McKersie (1986) have explained, labor relations is now a part of competitive strategy. This has led some companies to seek better relations with their unions, hoping that cooperation can create the needed gains in quality and productivity. Others have simply tried to avoid unions or crush those that already operate, convinced that unions inherently produce inefficiency and destroy their ability to compete. In either case labor negotiators now have less room to maneuver, public displays of conflict are more likely to result in full-blown exit strategies on the part of management, and the requirements for innovation and change may be far more than can be handled backstage. Where there is a fair amount of economic stability the traditional process may still suffice, but where there are sincere needs for more radical changes, the flaws of the traditional system loom large.

Kochan, Katz, and McKersie (1986) also point out that in many companies influence over labor relations and negotiations has shifted away from the labor relations professional and into the hands of both local line managers and top executives. These are people who may not know or care about the rituals of bargaining and do not have the kind of relationships with union leaders that established labor-relations managers had cultivated over the years. Where this has occurred, many of the mechanisms for backstage work may no longer be effective.

A sense of frustration with the existing approach to bargaining is apparent among many negotiators. As one union negotiator put it, labor and management have been trapped into having to play a game where each side tries to "beat the other down until we're sure we got all we could." Another complained that despite efforts by the company and the union to develop joint councils and other cooperative programs, "all of those positive things seem to disappear when we're in bargaining." And union leaders recognize that the old ways will no longer work: As several negotiators at Texas Bell put it while grimly considering their futures over drinks, "The days of the strike are gone." Strikes may happen, but they are not as likely as before to work out in the best interests of the union and therefore need to be deemphasized as a strategic option. Many negotiators on both sides feel that the existing rituals are too confining and the existing strategies too ineffective. They want change, and know that it is necessary, but do not have a clear sense of how to get there.[2]

---

2. Murray and Reshef (1988) argue that change is underway that is breaking down unions' old paradigm, but no new one has yet emerged to replace the old one.

As one union leader put it, "any contemporary manager or union leader realizes that their roles are changing."

Costs and Benefits

The current system of labor negotiations is both functional and flawed. In earlier chapters we saw the ways in which the traditional rituals of labor negotiation helps people manage an enormously complex social environment and provide leverage for the one party—labor—which depends on mobilization as a source of its power. Given the legal constraints of the labor negotiations framework, the unions' political structure, natural group dynamics, and the role expectations placed on bargainers, the rituals of bargaining are adaptive for the individuals involved. In this chapter we also saw the potential weaknesses of the traditional system: The public drama of conflict can become too dominant a part of the process, backstage contacts may not result in effective communication, and mistakes can be made. And the union side, in particular, is vulnerable when there are mistakes and misunderstandings. There is good reason for concerned observers to call for change. But any effort to create change has to be done with an awareness of the benefits of the traditional system and the forces that continue to make it sensible for negotiators to play their traditional roles. As long as the legal, political, and social pressures remain the same, we can expect labor negotiators to continually reinvent the traditional rituals of bargaining.

Case Studies of Change

The tension between change and stability is examined in part II. Each of the next four chapters presents a study of negotiations where the traditional process was altered in some ways. At New

Bell Publishing (chapter 6) negotiators managed to expand the boundaries of the backstage to include not just the lead bargainers but also most members of both negotiating teams. At International Harvester (chapter 7) management simply ignored the traditional rituals as they sought to change the culture of the company and revive its rapidly diminishing fortunes. At Midwestern University, Western Technologies, and Texas Bell (chapters 8 and 9), negotiators tried to adopt a "mutual gains" approach to negotiations. The stimulus for change varied in each of these cases: At NBP the changes emerged as negotiators shaped the process to meet their personal preferences, at IH the shift came inadvertently as a part of a more general strategy of organizational change, and at the other organizations the process was changed as a result of a conscious decision to try to make negotiations more productive and less acrimonious. But in each case the changes that were made ran in the face of traditional role expectations and left negotiators exposed to the same pressures that generated the traditional system in the first place. In each of these cases negotiators sought some benefits from change, many of which mirrored the flaws of the traditional system cited in this chapter, but they also confronted high costs to change, many of which mirrored the benefits of the traditional system discussed throughout part I. Taken together, the studies that follow provide examples of where pressures might come from for change and the benefits that are sought, while also pointing out some of the pitfalls that are associated with change and the forces that inhibit any effort to alter the roles and rituals of negotiations.

II

Transforming
Roles and Rituals:
Case Studies in Change

7

Managing around Roles: New Bell Publishing

Negotiators at the Minnesota table of New Bell Publishing developed a way of negotiating that differed markedly from typical negotiations: They publicly abided by the traditional roles and rituals of negotiations but privately escaped from them. They did this by, in effect, expanding the domain of the backstage—by finding ways for their entire bargaining teams, rather than just the lead bargainers, to meet away from the watchful eyes of observers and feel free, within the group, to step out of role. Away from the view of constituents, they shared information freely between the two teams, openly discussed issues and ideas, and dropped displays of labor-management acrimony. Freed from the constraints of a public performance, the two negotiating teams together became a joint team, with a common problem and a shared leadership. They played some of their traditional roles but managed their way around those roles.

The results of these negotiations were generally positive: Bargainers were able to arrive at an agreement, and they did not experience the high personal costs that can be associated with traditional, antagonistic bargaining. They were also able to engage in broad problem-solving discussions and use the ideas and contributions of most bargainers rather than just a few. At the same time, however, there was a cost to this approach: In the

process of minimizing constituents' influence (and their behavioral expectations), union members lost touch with them. As a
result some segments of the union felt isolated from the negotiation process and challenged the initial ratification vote. Moving
too much of the negotiations backstage can put negotiators in an
untenable position. While managing around roles offers an alternative for negotiating teams that trust each other, do not want to
engage in the traditional drama of conflict, and have the skill to
fend off outside monitoring, it is an approach that is not without
great risk as well.

New Bell Publishing

New Bell Publishing (NBP) produces Yellow Pages phone
books. Salespeople sell advertising space to businesses, clerical
staff people process the orders, and artists create the ads. The
final book is printed by an outside contractor. NBP covers six
states, three of which are organized by the United Telephone
Workers (UTW): Minnesota, Nebraska, and Iowa. Until 1984,
when the telecommunications industry was deregulated, this
business was part of AT&T. With the breakup of AT&T, NBP
was made into a subsidiary of one of the newly created Regional
Bell Operating Companies. At that point NBP's Yellow Pages
still dominated the regions they covered, but deregulation created new threats: Several new companies quickly entered the
Yellow Pages business in their markets, and each of the other
Bell Operating Companies were now potential competitors.
Compared to the days when AT&T had a monopoly, New Bell
Publishing had to compete more aggressively to keep market
share (still 90% in 1986) and hold down costs.

    The 1986 round of negotiations at NBP were its first since
deregulation and its first as a separate entity. The company was
concerned that its costs were out of line with those of local competitors (clerical workers were paid well over market rates) and

that its sales costs varied too much between different states. Therefore it sought to impose a wage freeze for clerical workers in all three states and lower commission payouts for salespeople in Iowa (they were paid approximately 20% more than their counterparts in Nebraska and Minnesota).

Since each state had different concerns, the company set up a decentralized negotiation structure, under which each of the three states would negotiate its own agreement. At the same time there was strong centralized control from the corporate office: The company's top HR manager, Matt Daniels, served as lead strategist and coordinator for the three tables, state-level negotiators were connected to the central office via computer ties, and each team went into negotiations with detailed strategic goals, prewritten language, and a series of planned offers and counteroffers that were in most cases common to all the tables. Martin Selly, the corporate labor relations manager for NBP, led the company's negotiating team in Minnesota, which also included a local sales manager and a local clerical (or publishing) manager.[1]

The concerns of the union also varied slightly in each state. More important, within each state, the union included two groups—salespeople and clerical workers—that had very different interests: Salespeople earned $30–$60,000 and were mostly white and male; clerical workers earned $15–$25,000 and were mostly female, many were black, and many were single parents. The assistant to the regional vice president of the UTW, Ben Hammond, was in charge of coordinating the union's bargaining strategy for all three states, but the negotiations themselves were conducted locally. Frances Avens, from the national UTW staff,

---

1. The company also assigned a note-taker to the team. This staff member was transferred to labor relations shortly before negotiations and quit shortly after them. She was not mentioned by any of the parties in the interviews and was apparently simply ignored during negotiations. She was, for all intents and purposes, not a member of the management team and will not be considered in this analysis.

led the union's team in Minnesota, which included a local representative from sales and one from publishing.

Neither side made a decision to consciously change the process of bargaining, but as negotiators in Minnesota worked together, an unusual pattern of interaction emerged. Instead of enacting the distinction between labor and management during negotiations, these negotiators only rarely felt compelled to display antagonism toward each other. Relationships developed that were as strong across the table as on the same side. Instead of maintaining strict control, the lead bargainers allowed a looser, shared leadership structure to emerge. And instead of playing to the constituent audience, they tried to keep constituents away from negotiations and maintain as much freedom as possible from their behavioral expectations. They did not find themselves locked into the roles that typically dominate negotiations.

The following sections describe this unusual pattern of interactions, show how it came about, and examine the impact it had on these negotiations.

Informal Relations and Emergent Patterns of Leadership

At the Minnesota negotiations, relations between negotiators (listed in figure 7.1) deviated a great deal from the usual pattern. Martin Selly was the lead bargainer for the company, but his team had mixed feelings about him. Dan Bently (the publishing manager on the company's team) described him as a person who "came out of a UAW, hard-line, nail them to the wall, kind of environment." This approach, according to Bently, made Selly stand apart at the bargaining table: "There was a certain combination of personalities—Elon Yatteau, myself, and Jim and Frances that just seemed to work. And I might say *in spite of* Martin, because I don't think Martin was or is of the same ilk that we were, in that he is more stiff, formal."

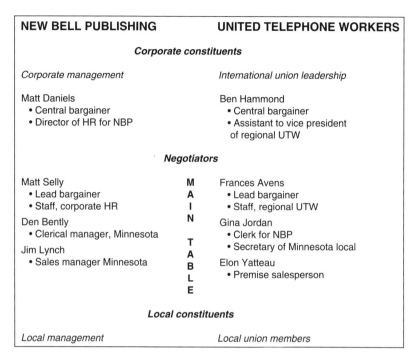

Figure 7.1
Formal structure and personnel at Minnesota table

Selly was a "challenge" to all the negotiators. Bently explained that Selly "took stands" that "we knew he was going to back off" from. But, he added, "It would take him *forever* to back off." Selly's approach was taken in stride:

> Jim and I would look at each other and we'd look at Yatteau, and we'd look up in the air and we'd kind of giggle at each other. We'd take a break and we'd come back and Martin had changed his position, and Jim and Yatteau and I would sit there and giggle and laugh because we knew what was going on.

Avens, the union's lead negotiator, was also somewhat frustrated with Selly but managed the situation with firmness and humor. She explained:

> Selly and I got into a few little rounds, but I guess that's just the nature of the whole thing. Martin used to make statements that when he bargained

before, people threw chairs out of the window. Martin and I got to the point that I told him I would take him and the chair and throw it out the window. But even though we were at odds a lot of times, I tried not to let that cause friction to the point that we couldn't negotiate next time. . . . I would have his people, Martin's people, sit on my side of the table before Martin would come in. I'd say, "Martin, you're bargaining by yourself, 'cause I've already got the people here on my side." We did try to make things light.

Selly understood his situation and felt comfortable with it. Even though he was teased by Avens, he felt that their relationship was "outstanding." He explained, "I liked her because she was very open, very direct. She used to kid me a lot at the bargaining table—she's got a pretty good sense of humor." Selly recognized that he "didn't really have what I would consider a real good relationship with Dan," his own teammate, but he also recognized that Bently was "a real asset during bargaining" because he was able to build a good relationship with his union counterpart in publishing, Gina Jordan.

The negotiators allowed Selly to maintain his formal authority—Bently was careful not to undercut Selly—yet Bently, Yatteau, Lynch, and Avens managed to discount, ignore, and work around the formal pattern of interactions that Selly brought to negotiations. While Selly remained formally in control on the management side, Bently emerged as an informal leader for all of the negotiators. While Selly concentrated on the task of bargaining, Bently helped the group maintain its interpersonal ties and emotional balance.[2]

Frances Avens, in contrast to Selly, acquired broader influence than could be attributed to her formal role as lead bargainer. She guided her team through the task of bargaining, but also became an informal, social leader for all of the negotiators. In terms of

---

2. In the words of Bales and Slater (1955), Selly remained the "task leader," namely the person who made sure that the group focused on what it needed to accomplish, showed up on time, and did its work in a timely and effective manner, while Bently became the group's "socioemotional leader," namely the person who made sure that the group had time to know, accept, and support each other.

task leadership, she made sure that the union team was clear about what it wanted. She explained:

When we sat at the table, this is what I did: If Martin brought something up, I'd say [to my team], "Can you live with that?" And if they said, "Yes," then I'd say, "Tell me why." If they said, "No," I'd say, "Then tell him why—tell Martin why we can't live with this kind of agreement."

She could also be extremely tough when something unfair occurred. In one early incident Selly commented that if the union struck, the company could assign salespeople to work in Tilden—an area that was not unionized and that needed more salespeople. At the time public relations people were videotaping the negotiations, and Selly was trying to be controversial. As Avens explained:

I raised hell. Because I said, "This is not bargaining in good faith." I got up and left the room. I was really angry, and in fact I went down and called my boss, and I told him I didn't want to bargain with Selly anymore because they're not bargaining in good faith. We're sitting at the table trying to get a contract, and he's talking about making scabs out of my people, to send them to Tilden to work. I don't think there's any faith or confidence there.

Avens also kept the group together emotionally. After the "big blowout" over Tilden salespeople, Avens explained, "We made Martin pay for good, we made him take us to a good restaurant." Avens was known for adding a sense of humor to negotiations. In one incident she told Selly to send Matt Daniels, the corporate human resources director, a message over the computer:

I said to Selly, "I want you to send Matt a message. I want you to tell him that if we reach an agreement, then he would have to pay the cost of unused picket signs purchased by the union in 1986." We put it on the machine and we all went in the room and listened [on the speakerphone]. Matt says, "Martin, what the hell is this?" So Martin says, "I'm sorry, Matt. This is what Frances says she has to have." He says, "Bullshit!" We all laughed!

"I tried," she said, "to make a game out of some of this because the stress was so bad."

Avens was held in very high regard by nearly everyone at the bargaining table. Jim Lynch reflected the sentiment on the management side:

She was very supportive in terms of *her* positions, but also when *we* discussed things, and it made sense, she understood and agreed. She wanted to make things happen and say, "Fine, that's good, now let's go on to something else." So she was very cooperative and a very high-class lady, and really wanted to accomplish the objective that we were there for.

On the union side, Elon Yatteau supported Avens (although he worried about her understanding of the sales job). Only Jordan did not get along with Avens. According to Selly, "Gina had never been a supporter of Frances. They had some kind of a rift between them going back a few years, so that's why she had a problem from time to time with Gina." Jordan was kept involved in the group primarily through her ties with Dan Bently. She said, "I felt very comfortable with Dan and I think that Dan put forth an honest effort to try and resolve the issues we discussed." In the end, she felt that people at the bargaining table "developed a mutual respect for one another."

In these negotiations some of the strongest relationships occurred between people on opposite sides of the table. In addition to the Selly-Avens and Bently-Jordan relationships, another strong tie across the bargaining table was between Yatteau and Lynch, the union and management representatives for sales. Lynch explained that he "disclosed and shared everything" with Yatteau. Lynch saw himself as a "subject matter expert" and felt that "Elon recognized it." At the same time Yatteau was "very helpful" to Lynch and was seen by him as "a super guy—you could discuss things with him."

Breaking out of Role

In these negotiations traditional role structures were not maintained: Ties among negotiators were enhanced, while those with constituents were downplayed; strong relationships developed across the bargaining table among all negotiators; leadership responsibilities were shared among other negotiators than just the lead bargainers. As a result the traditional role structure was overshadowed by a sense that negotiators on both sides had a common task, shared a common experience, and formed into a common group.

The most salient boundary was not between opposing negotiators but between these negotiators and outsiders. When Selly played along with Avens' practical joke on Matt Daniels over the phone, Selly's boss was the outsider to the negotiating group while Selly was an insider. A boundary line was drawn around the people who negotiated at the table. Avens reinforced this boundary by limiting outside reports. She cautioned everyone that "everything stays in this work group until we've got something tangible to give the people." She explained that "you lose a certain amount of trust, or create more mistrust on both sides, if you give a daily report of what's happening." Maintaining this boundary took some concerted effort, since outsiders continually wanted to find out about the negotiations. Yatteau explained:

All the time, [the salespeople] wanted to know what was happening. You'd go back to your office and there'd be guys lined up there saying, "Come on, tell us what's going on.". . . Phone calls, you name it. . . . We'd tell them flat out that bargaining is a "secret situation" and the biggest reason is because [neither] the company nor the union can afford to have the contract bargained at any place except at the bargaining table.

When outsiders did intrude, such as the time when public relations filmed the negotiations, it changed how they negotiated. With an external audience of a camera crew added to the negotiations, Selly played to their expectations by behaving as a tough antagonistic bargainer. Most of the time negotiators in Minnesota did manage to keep out external observers and buffer themselves from constituents' behavioral role expectations. In this way they were freed somewhat from the constraints of acting like representatives.

Within the group, as well, formal roles were not strictly enforced. While Selly was the formal leader of his team, others were allowed to and did emerge as informal and social leaders of the group. Dan Bently became an emotional leader for negotiators on both sides, and Avens became an informal leader for the group as a whole. Thus the typical strict hierarchy of control within teams was loosened a great deal.

Finally, any fault lines that did exist in this group did not match the formal divide between labor and management: There was as much positive affect and professional respect across the table as there was within teams. The stronger divisions were within the teams: between Avens and Jordan, and between Bently and Selly.

Changing the Rituals

The changes in role structure that emerged during the Minnesota negotiations allowed these negotiators to spend less time presenting the typical drama of conflict, and more time engaging in discussions of the type usually reserved for lead bargainers in sidebar meetings.

Traditional Rituals

To a certain degree these negotiators continued to enact the traditional rituals of negotiations. As we saw above, Selly felt that in his role as lead bargainer he had to start with a tough position and only then back off and accept the deal that he knew he would offer in the first place. And, when the cameras were there, he felt he had to behave in a traditional manner. The need for such "game playing" was a source of great frustration for Yatteau, who thought that, "After a year of prebargaining, it wasn't necessary to go through the theatrics of bargaining." Meanwhile Avens acted tough for Jordan. As Bently put it,

Avens did the typical "mating dance" that "a good union leader should go through at the table, and that's to sit there and say, 'There is no way in hell we're going to take that new health insurance.'" He explained that Avens "would sit there and pound the table and really be talking strong that she's 'not going to do this,' and Gina would be sitting there saying, 'Yeah, yeah,' agreeing with her totally."

But in each of these cases most of the negotiators knew to discount these acts. Yatteau, Bently, and Lynch giggled together at Selly's tough-guy act, and when Avens pounded the table for Jordan, everyone else, according to Bently, was "sitting there knowing that the show she is putting on was for Gina" so that when an agreement was reached, "Jordan would be able to say, 'I did everything I could do.'" They understood that to a certain degree, Avens, Jordan, and Selly had to play to their constituents or their own images of their role in negotiations. The rituals of bargaining did not interfere with relationships between bargainers. Jordan commented, "Sometimes we fought—a dog and cat fight, you know. Then there were those times when we laughed together, we went out and had lunch together."

Dropping the Facade: Negotiating as Sidebar Discussions

In addition to discounting the public performances, these negotiators spent a great deal of time interacting informally. As usual there were sidebar meetings between the two lead bargainers (this, Selly explained, was where much of the "real bargaining occurs"). But not just the lead bargainers met informally: There were many informal, sidebarlike contacts between other negotiators as well. As Lynch described: "We'd start every morning [with] a nice little social half-hour with coffee and doughnuts. And we generally went to lunch twice a week as a team, both the union and us." These informal interactions helped build trust between the two sides and provided a place for negotiators to express their views more openly. Bently described the role of the video game room in negotiations:

> We would walk into that room and start playing this golf game and just be chatting about the problems. We were able to say things like, "this person is a dumb shit" or "that one is," and "we've got work to do and they're screwing up." This is the union and management talking together. We were able to recognize each other's position and the difficulties that others encountered. It was a matter of talking about it on a man-to-man basis rather than in a formal environment behind a table or something.

Throughout negotiations, they were quick to break up into smaller groups where they could talk about problems and ideas one-on-one. Selly described the pattern:

> We'd make our formal presentations at the bargaining table; we'd go through the contract language, and we'd tentatively agree to the contract language at the bargaining table. Then, usually after three or four hours, we'd spend the rest of the afternoon in subcommittees. I would go off with Frances, and Bently would go with Gina Jordan, and Jim Lynch would go with Elon Yatteau.

The sidebar style of interacting that permeated these negotiations was carried to the main table as well: Even there discussions were open, and all negotiators were involved. As Yatteau put it, "Across the table, everybody talked. It wasn't one of those where I'd whisper to him and he'd whisper to you and then he would finally say it."

The process that developed was one that allowed everyone to participate and contribute: No one was uninvolved or bored. Each negotiator worked with his or her opposite in areas where he or she was an expert. And throughout the negotiations channels of communication were kept open. There was a certain amount of playing to the audience in these negotiations, but negotiators mostly limited outside interference and discouraged the attitudes and behaviors typical of negotiations. They did not solve all problems, but they were able to engage in a problem-solving process.

Expanding the Influence of Trust

Just as lead bargainer contacts are based on and help build trust and credibility, the open discussions that occurred between negotiators in Minnesota were also based on trust and credibility. Dan Bently, in a letter to Martin Selly after negotiations, expressed his opinion that in addition to having good staff support and being well prepared, the most important factor in their ability to handle the negotiations was the "development of a constructive, positive, cooperative bargaining environment." He wrote:

> This is a tough one to define for future reference but absolutely essential. I felt that our Minnesota Team (both Union and Management) felt good about what we were doing, how we were going about it, and showed respect for each other's views and positions. I feel that a lot of what we accomplished was due to the genuine good feelings and respect that we had for each other as individuals. Much of this was accomplished on break, lunchtime and after hours. We got to know each other personally and this contributed substantially to our success. Could this have been a detriment if we had reached an impasse? I think not. We had several serious, critical situations when we could have lost it all. I feel that our positive, constructive attitudes helped us reach a successful conclusion [dated August 7, 1986].

The Outcome

On July 9, 1986, the NBP contract expired. Three days later, after a contract extension, Minnesota reached a tentative agreement; each of the other two unionized states had strikes for many weeks. As Selly put it, the relationships they developed among negotiators at Minnesota "probably had something to do with the reason that we were the only table out of the three to successfully negotiate agreement without a strike."

But the final days of negotiations and the ratification process were rather rocky. What happened in these last days gives us a sense of the limits of managing around roles. While the negotiators might have been able to fend off outside observers and their role expectations during much of negotiations, that proved impossible to sustain as the contract expiration date drew near. While they were able to explore ideas and discuss issues when there was plenty of time left, the pressures of a deadline made such discussions impossible. And, although negotiators in Minnesota had worked together largely as an independent unit, external constituents intruded more and more on the negotiating group. Much of what occurred in the final days was in response to outside forces, including pressures from Daniels at corporate headquarters and from a group of salespeople who were keeping an eye on Yatteau's actions. As Selly explained:

> We were down to the eleventh hour on the commission plan. I called up Matt Daniels and told him that we just couldn't nail down the final details on the plan—that the union basically wanted some time to think about it. And Daniels said, "Bullshit. You get back in there. I want an agreement now. I've already been in contact with our corporate communication department, we've been in contact with the newspapers. As soon as those newspapers hit the street this morning, they're going to say: 'New Bell Publishing in Minnesota Reaches an Agreement on a Contract.'" I said, "OK." So I got hold of Jim Lynch, and we went marching down to Elon Yatteau's hotel room and pounded on the door. Elon comes walking to the door, he's in his underwear and he's groggy. He said, "What the hell do you guys want?" We go marching into his room, and I said, "Goddamit Elon, we need an agreement right now!" We had all the data—all our numbers on the commission plans—and I said, "Here, take a look at this again. This is the best we can do. We need an agreement. I'm not leaving until I get one." So he goes back and looks at the numbers, squinting. Finally he just lays down on his bed, puts his papers over his head, and says "I can't believe you guys are doing this to me. These are Gestapo tactics." So I said, "Elon, we gotta have an agreement."

That night they made an agreement, but the next morning Yatteau met with several salespeople who served as advisers and was told that the contract was unacceptable. According to Matt Daniels, the company realized at the same time that the deal was no good, so that when "Elon called up and said he couldn't live with it, I said, 'Fine.'" As Selly described the situation:

I got a call about 6:30 in the morning from Elon, and he said, "The deal is off!" I go, "What do you mean the deal is off?" He said, "The deal's off! I had a chance to look at those numbers, and we're going to end up losing money under this plan. It will never sell." So we got everyone back together again . . . and we wrapped it up by about 4 or 5 o'clock."

But the problem of "selling the contract" remained. Both sides were aware that an unsuccessful presentation to the membership could cause the contract to not be ratified. Bently helped Jordan master the numbers in the contract:

I spent the majority of my time dealing with Gina on how to sell it to the union . . . going through by name, by individual, their wage treatment based on the new contract and showing her how many people were going to get increases. I gave her a complete package which she in turn [used in the ratification] meetings to convince the publishing union members that this was the right thing to do.

And Lynch helped Avens master the part of the contract that dealt with the salespeople:

I spent an awful lot of time with Frances, making sure she understood perfectly what I was saying, what it meant to the salespeople, earning potential, etc.

Despite the preparation that the committee made to present the contract, several behind-the-scenes leaders among the salespeople opposed the new contract. Avens felt that Yatteau had made a mistake by discussing the terms of the contract with others in the final days: These salespeople knew enough to make trouble but not enough to represent the contract accurately.

Shortly after the tentative agreement was reached, the clerical workers voted overwhelmingly to ratify the contract. Voting continued the next day for the salespeople. Avens, hearing that there might be trouble, came to the meeting to count the votes. During that meeting, one politically powerful salesman gave an impassioned speech against the contract. When the votes for the two days were counted, a majority supported the contract, so it was ratified. But the salespeople knew from an informal count that most of *them* had voted against it. Therefore some salespeople challenged the vote count and the process of mixing the clerical and sales votes. They complained that too many salespeople were on vacation at the time of the vote and insisted that a new vote be taken among them the next week. A new vote was taken and, after some internal political battles, the International UTW recognized the procedural and numerical accuracy of Avens's final count.

Limits of Managing around Roles

The very independence from constituents that helped the negotiators work well as an independent unit came to haunt them in the end. As Yatteau put it, the "emotional hook" used by the opposition salespeople was that:

> They were kept in the dark and they resented it. They resented the fact that we didn't come out every day and say, "Here's what's happening, folks. What do you think?" . . . We were "deceiving" them. The word got out that we were in bed with the company . . . that we were stabbing them in the back, . . . that we weren't looking after their best interests.

As Avens saw it, the problem was that there was not quite *enough* secrecy: If negotiations were kept airtight, then the negative rumors would not have happened. She argued, "I think one of the mistakes Elon made was he was keeping some other people involved in negotiations a little bit more than he should have." Yet they were already pushing the limits of what was acceptable. The negotiators were representatives, and constituents felt that they had a right to know what was happening. At least one negotiator, Gina Jordan, felt that maintaining secrecy kept her from doing her job:

> It was more or less like we could not discuss this with the rank and file. . . . I was their representative, elected by them, and I should have been giving them a daily update of bargaining. . . . I couldn't. I was told that I couldn't by the UTW.

In the end negotiators had to deal with the reality that it was still outsiders who had ultimate authority. If Daniels made a decision that the company's offer was final, the company team had to abide by that; if the union membership rallied against an agreed-upon clause, the deal would not be ratified. This created frustration among negotiators on both sides. Lynch complained about Yatteau's inability to make independent decisions. And Yatteau complained that Lynch understood his perspective on the sales commission plans being discussed, but it was Daniels, a nonsalesman, who made the final decisions. While the negotiators at the table had developed a relationship and a sense of trust, this had not occurred among those away from the table. One of the salespeople, who got involved at the end and had not developed a relationship with the company's negotiators, had a very different view of Jim Lynch than Yatteau did:

I always had a feeling about Jim. He's a good salesman . . . [but] I always felt like when I was [meeting] with him, he wasn't hearing a damn thing I was saying. . . . He would go back to his [management] guys and say, "These [union] guys maybe got a point, but you guys do what you want to." I didn't trust him that far.

These negotiators could avoid the strict behavioral constraints of their roles during much of negotiations, but ultimately they had to abide by the dictates of constituents and act as conduits for their views. They could develop a process of interacting that was nonantagonistic and creative, but that process could not be sustained into the final, pressured days of bargaining.

Anatomy of Change

Despite these problems negotiators in Minnesota were able to come to an agreement without a strike, while the other two states were not. The process was much more open and direct than is typical of labor negotiations. How did this happen?

Expanding the Backstage

These negotiators were able to create a context where much of the negotiation occurred backstage. The group as a whole was able to buffer itself from outside observations, just as lead bargainers traditionally do when talking among themselves. They did this by keeping outsiders from intruding on the negotiations, and by defining negotiators as "insiders" and others as "outsiders."

In addition they knew to discount traditional behaviors when they did occur. To a certain degree negotiators played traditional roles because they thought that some members of the team expected it (i.e., Gina Jordan) or because they expected that of themselves (i.e., Martin Selly). But these behaviors were not taken seriously by others most of the time.

Beyond discounting, they knew to actually move away from the formal setting of the main table and allow conversations to continue—over lunch, while playing video games, and during one-on-one subcommittee meetings. If there was any sense of playing to an audience at the main table, it was mitigated by these efforts to move away from the main table. Much of the time they spent together was in off-stage settings similar to those that are usually inhabited only by lead bargainers.

By buffering themselves from outside influences, collectively discounting rituals, and including the entire teams in sidebarlike meetings, the Minnesota negotiators effectively pushed back the boundaries of the backstage. Whereas typically the backstage is inhabited only by lead bargainers, here it was inhabited by all the negotiators (see figure 7.2).

Informal Leadership

The negotiators were able to develop a different leadership pattern. Inside the expanded backstage, those who were most articulate, experienced, and charismatic came to be highly respected among *all* of the negotiators and served, in effect, as leaders for the entire group. These leaders were not necessarily those who held formal roles as lead bargainers (Avens was a lead bargainer while Bently was not); rather, they emerged as leaders only in the process of negotiating. Compared to most negotiations, the lead bargainers in Minnesota did not defend their authority by keeping other leaders from emerging, and neither the formal nor the emergent leaders felt they had to dominate the negotiations; everyone was allowed to participate in the conversation.

These two factors—leadership and an expanded backstage—are highly related. Lead bargainers are likely to feel less pressure to act out the role of lead bargainer if they face less scrutiny by

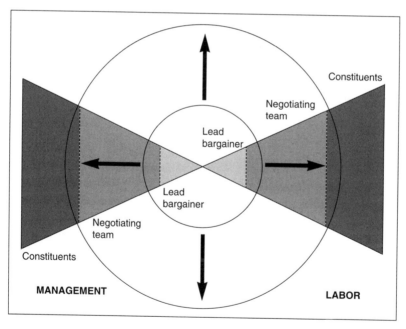

Figure 7.2
Expanding the backstage

constituents. At the same time, if leaders emerge among the negotiators, they are likely to feel secure in their authority and more comfortable acting independently of constituents.

Redefining the "Group"

Without the external pressures to enact the labor-management opposition and with the presence of a shared leadership, these negotiators could, more than is typical in labor negotiations, act as a united group with a common problem and a common identity; in this sense they served as a "joint" bargaining team rather than as two groups interacting at arm's length across the bargaining table (see figure 7.3).

Personal Skills

Another important but highly intangible factor in this case was personal characteristics and skills. Avens knew how to manage a

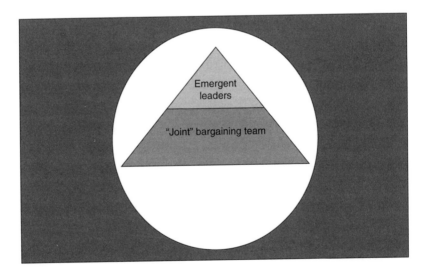

Figure 7.3
Inside the expanded backstage

group so that it focused on the issues, and she was able to get the team members to make decisions. She also knew that it was important to limit outside influences and helped the group to see itself as a joint team. Lastly she knew how to break the tensions inherent in negotiations so that the group could continue to function together productively. These skills led others to respect her, and her sense of humor led others to like her. Given this respect and her experience, she had enough confidence that it was not necessary to control every interaction between the two sides.

Selly's personality also played a role. If he had had a greater personal need for control, he might not have allowed others to contribute as much and might have pushed harder to dominate as the lead bargainer. It helped that he respected his teammates, Lynch and Bently, as experts who knew their areas better than he did and people who were willing to put a great deal of effort into the negotiations. They had much to contribute, and he let them do so.

Bently was also a key player. He was the one person, more than any other, who found it easy to respect and understand managers and union members alike. And it helped that none of the union negotiators were politically ambitious; if any had been, they might have brought to the table expectations that others should behave antagonistically, or they might have enacted a drama of conflict to boost their popularity with constituents. All of the Minnesota negotiators approached negotiations with a basic desire to be helpful, a willingness to let the leaders drive the process, and an interest in talking with the other side. Again, these tendencies were probably enhanced by the leadership style that emerged during negotiations and the sense that negotiations were backstage much of the time.

Blind Luck and Interpersonal "Chemistry"

Finally, not just individual personalities mattered but how they mixed with each other. Bently thought that it was "blind luck to have personalities that matched." Selly thought that "it just seemed like we had the right chemistry, all of us as a group." But for Jordan the relationships were as much a result of the process as the cause of it: "We developed, from bargaining, a mutual respect for one another. Once we left there, we viewed folks differently than we had going in . . . because in the contact that we had and the disagreements that we had, it kind of bonded us."

Managing around Roles

The NBP case identifies one set of strategies that can help negotiators escape the role constraints of labor negotiations: create more backstage interactions among negotiators, buffer the teams from outside monitoring, allow natural leaders to emerge, and forge a joint team. But these changes are not easy to achieve. It may be difficult to keep people off the bargaining teams who feel a need to grandstand, especially on the union side where representatives are chosen through a political process. Lead bargainers may not have enough confidence in their skills or status to allow a joint team to emerge. And it is probably impossible to foresee how individual personalities will interact. Moreover this approach is inherently limited even where it can be achieved. As we saw in this case, constituents will probably become more active toward the end of negotiations, so buffering cannot be sustained throughout the process. More important, the kinds of behavior seen in Minnesota are still not considered legitimate by outsiders. Negotiators risk losing credibility if their actions are discovered. The strategy of managing around roles allows negotiators to escape some of the expectations that are placed on them, but it does not change those expectations.

8

Ignoring Roles and Rituals: International Harvester

After 20 years of gradual deterioration International Harvester began the decade the of the 1970s with an effort to reinvent itself: It restructured the company, brought in new management, and cut costs. By the end of the decade it was time to address the inefficiencies that resulted from the restrictive contract with the UAW and change the tone and direction of labor relations for the company. IH approached the 1979 negotiations with the goal of changing work rules and changing its relationship with the union. Archie McCardell, the company's CEO, described its goals:[1]

> We told ourselves that as long as we can make progress in at least one [area], that would establish the parameters that we could then work on in future negotiations. . . . We just wanted to make enough progress that we could establish . . . the principle that, for the first time in 40-odd years, . . . their contract ought to be a two-way street, and we could in fact get something.

To achieve this goal, the company approached the negotiation process in a very different way. Partly out of choice and partly because those put in charge of negotiations did not know the traditional roles and rituals of labor negotiations, it made the negotiations more formal: It eliminated sidebar discussions, did not

---

1. These quotes come from my interview with Mr. McCardell.

signal, and stayed at the main table. It would not go through the old rituals, play the old roles, or engage in backstage interactions. IH told the union exactly what it wanted and expected from day one, rather than playing the "game." The negotiators would, as they saw it, simply be more straightforward and approach negotiations like "rational," reasonable people.

Keeping negotiations on the front stage and ignoring traditional roles and rituals had several unforseen effects: (1) it eliminated the company's ability to correctly interpret the union's concerns, positions, and emotions; (2) it eliminated the union's ability to correctly interpret the company's own concerns, positions, and emotions; (3) it eliminated the union's lead bargainers' ability to maintain control over their bargaining team; and as a result (4) negotiations devolved into a direct confrontation between the two sides, unmediated by negotiators. There may be conditions where these outcomes are desirable, intended, or minimally damaging; current research on labor negotiations has explored the times and conditions when confrontation or "forcing" is desired (Walton, Cutcher-Gershenfeld, and McKersie, forthcoming). In the Harvester case the results were disastrous: An expected strike turned into an unexpected six-month long battle that cost the company $200 million and contributed to the demise of this industrial giant.

The Harvester case is no doubt extreme: It represents an extraordinarily clumsy attempt at change. Since then companies that needed change have been careful either to develop a more cooperative stance toward unions when they can not avoid them, or to push in no uncertain terms to destroy them. With the economy reeling in the 1980s and collective lessons learned from IH, few would blunder so skillessly into the kind of quagmire that is documented in this chapter. Moreover, with their backs against the wall from economic and political pressures in the 1980s, unions are probably more likely to relent than the UAW did at Harvester. Nonetheless, this case shows how difficult it is to ignore a system of social interaction when the parties involved are still cast in traditional roles, and still expect the traditional rituals and depend on them. While some may, by nature or strategy, want to bring a kind of simple rationality to negotiations, doing so leaves unresolved many of the social and political pressures that are an inherent part of negotiations. Attempts to rationalize the negotiation process away may, paradoxically, make the process more rather than less unpredictable.

Problems at IH and a New Leadership in the 1970s

Prior to the 1970s Harvester was considered an industrial giant, and employees felt that a job at Harvester meant security for life. Managers knew that any product they made could be easily sold, so they managed their factories to avoid disruption—it was important to maintain high levels of output so that orders could be filled. Through the 1960s the company held on to its large share of the market, but due to its overconfidence and commitment to high and stable dividend payments, there was little investment in plants and products.[2] Some of its new tractors and construction equipment were plagued with breakdowns, and IH's technological reputation began to sink. At the same time profits declined as a result of its costly, top-heavy administrative structure, outdated plants, high wages, and restrictive work rules.[3]

When Brooks McCormick took over the company's reins in 1971, "he recognized that the company's tradition-bound organization had lost vitality and grown complacent" (Marsh 1985, 131). As one member of Harvester's board put it, "It was clear at

2. In the 1970s Harvester's investment for all of its businesses—farm machinery, trucks, construction equipment, and other activities—fell below the amount that Caterpillar invested for construction equipment alone (Marsh and Saville 1982).
3. For the decade of the 1960s Harvester's profit margins averaged 3.1%, while Deer's averaged 5.6% and Caterpillar's averaged 7.9% (Marsh and Saville 1982).

the time that the company needed a radical change, that just evolution wouldn't take care of the problems in the amount of time that we had to correct them." McCormick set in motion a series of changes designed to put IH back on the road to financial health. He restructured the company, hired outsiders so that there would be some "new blood" in Harvester's inbred bureaucracy, and planned to eventually extract the company from the costly "traditions" of labor relations that had evolved over the years.

"Fresh blood" was needed because, as one executive put it, "The old Harvester management had basically accepted this level of performance." Current managers were too friendly with each other and too familiar with IH to be able to make any abrupt changes. A member of Harvester's board explained the board's view:

Something radical [was] needed in the company [to] shake it out of its lethargy . . . Somebody that's grown up within it would find it very difficult to do that. The inside people were pretty good, but they would carry on the same tradition.

When McCormick retired, he wanted an outside manager to replace him. Archie McCardell, a Xerox executive, was chosen. He, in turn, brought in more new people, including a new chief operating officer, Warren Hayford, and a new vice president of human resources, Grant Chandler. McCardell, like McCormick, wanted outsiders who were not steeped in the old traditions of the company. His new hires knew this and chose not to learn those old traditions and bad habits. Hayford explained:

I think it's easy to pick up on the culture and language of any company. If you don't want to change things, then you understand the culture and the language; if you want to change things, then you don't understand the culture and language.

As soon as McCardell joined IH in 1977, he began aggressive cost cutting; he increased common parts across lines and cut

2,600 middle managers as well as 150 of the company's corporate staff (Marsh 1985, 182). He used the savings to invest in plant modernization and R&D. He also took a tougher stance against the union. When several local strikes occurred, the company did not give in; IH engaged in prolonged negotiations with the one local where the strike was legal, and imposed stiff disciplinary actions on those who engaged in wildcat strikes.

The 1979 Negotiations

The company's aggressive stance toward the union carried over into the 1979 negotiations. According to one plant manager:

As we approached negotiations, you could feel the determination of the company to make headway. It became clear we were going to step out of character. Before, we would surrender to their demands. In 1979, we attempted to take control of negotiations and put forward our demands.

The company decided that it would have to follow the economic "pattern" set in the UAW's negotiations with other companies, but in return it had to get a number of work rule concessions from the union.

Changes in Process

To achieve these goals, the company approached negotiations in a very different way. First, the negotiators addressed only a handful of items in these negotiations and did not let them "fall off the table." As the company's chief negotiator, Grant Chandler, put it, "[the company] did not want to take pages and pages of demands in there. We wanted to just be able to talk about something over and over again." Another top executive added: "We didn't go in there with a laundry list. We tried to create the perception, which we felt was fact, that we didn't want to just muddle up the process with 50 demands, knowing full well maybe half of them didn't mean anything." They brought to the table a request for seven work rule changes, including two that would later provide the rallying cry for union resistance: a clause requiring workers to work overtime when the company requested it (called "mandatory overtime") and changes of job transfer rules. These items were chosen based on the belief that they would not cost workers anything and were items that the UAW had accepted at competitors' plants.

Second, they would be very direct about what they would give the union. They decided to announce up front that the company would match the wage pattern set in Detroit. According to Chandler:

> We were setting the stage that said, "Hey, we know—we *know*—that unless we take a long strike from you folks, we are going to have to give you the same financial package that you've gotten out of other companies." . . . Believe me, when you sit at the bargaining table and you know what all of those corporations have given, you are not going to give anything different.

Therefore, according to McCardell, "We told the union from day one that we would meet whatever the pattern was [but that] we wanted some changes in work practices."

Third, the negotiators wanted to make negotiations more formal and businesslike. The company requested that the negotiations no longer be held at the Drake Hotel but rather in a conference room on the first floor of Harvester's office building built specifically for that purpose. This would remove the "social" atmosphere of negotiations and save money. "If you're talking in terms of a company not making a lot of money or not being able to keep a lot of money, being more economical in the process of negotiations couldn't hurt that kind of impression," said an IH executive. A local manager, as well, noticed the company's more businesslike approach to negotiations, "My view at that point was that the company was better organized and really was approaching the contract negotiations more from a business fashion that year than any other year." As one manager put it, "We tried to change the whole thing. Consciously, we wanted to change the whole tone to make it more businesslike."

These changes led to others, such as the lack of sidebar discussions. An IH executive described the situation:

I don't think there was an intent or a stated purpose of eliminating sidebars. On the other hand, when you have a commitment to 5 or 6 or 7 objectives, it's a lot different than when you have 25, 30, up to 60. So I think it was intended definitely that the significant negotiations were going to occur at the main table, . . . there [would] not be a lot of side meetings or discussions.

This restriction of contacts to a formal setting was also, in the opinion of some managers I interviewed, a function of Chandler's discomfort with informal interactions and his highly formal style.

Finally, the company's direct and honest approach was taken to the extreme in one, probably unplanned, comment. In the opening session the company's spokesman, Warren Mortonson, made an off-the-cuff remark that the seven issues presented to the union "are here today, will be there tomorrow, and will be there when the strike begins." It was common knowledge within management that the changes would result in a strike, but not a six-month-long strike. Chandler thought the strike might last three or four months; McCardell prepared for a two-month strike, expecting that there would be no incentive for the union to come back until the holidays—if workers came back before Christmas, they would receive their allotted paid vacation days.

Changes in Personnel

This new approach to bargaining developed because new people were put in charge of the process. Using the same logic that led McCormick to bring in McCardell, McCardell made Grant

Chandler the lead bargainer. He was new to IH, to the UAW, and to large-scale negotiations. "From that point of view," explained one company manager, "he had a deficiency in understanding the UAW. On the other hand, possibly having a big understanding might have inhibited him from doing what he understood his job to be." Other managers noted his lack of understanding of the union, "I always felt that Grant, because of his newness to the situation or whatever, never had that intimate feel of, knowledge, or sensitivity—understanding—of the other side." Years later, in response to comments like this, Chandler would explain:

That was not my responsibility [to understand the union]. It was the responsibility of the person who had the labor-relations spot. The negotiation strategy and the negotiation decisions were my responsibility, along with making recommendations to executive management.

The company's chief spokesman under Chandler was from IH, but he was, like Chandler, new to negotiations, as were the four group HR directors on the team. There were a few old hands, but they held little sway. One top executive explained that McCardell did not trust their views:

Those were the same guys, other than Grant Chandler, who had kind of caved in and took a very soft and ineffectual position with the UAW for a number of years. I think Archie felt that, while he would listen to what they had to say, he wasn't going to let them control the tone or direction.

At the time McCardell explained that, for the moment, he had delegated all responsibilities to subordinates *except* that of running the labor negotiations (Hamermesh and Christiansen 1985).

Thus the company's negotiators broke from the past rituals of bargaining, partly because they were not loyal to the rituals and partly because they simply did not know them. In either case they took a bargaining strategy that the old-hand bargainers did not agree with, which they thought would have disastrous consequences, and which would not have been used if a new team were not in charge.

An Outline of Events

Negotiations began on August 9. The company explained that it needed to make IH more competitive and indicated that it would not drop its demands for work rule changes but added that "we are not a Chrysler, and we don't hope for a substandard agreement."[4] The union called for "progress" in wages and benefits, and cited cost-of-living adjustments for retired workers as "the number one issue in this year's round of bargaining."[5] Two weeks later negotiations began in earnest, and each side traded position papers. In September the contract was extended a month to allow the UAW to focus on its other negotiations, with Ford, GM, and Chrysler. But as the new November 1 deadline drew near, the two sides were still far apart. By mid-October the union's negotiations bulletins began to reflect frustration with the company's bargaining tactics. One such report (October 12, 1979) read:

The Company's message was loud and clear. *They said that they had no plans now nor in the future to meet with us or to give us an economic package unless we accept their demands on mandatory overtime, pieceworkers' rights, qualifications for holiday pay, etc.* As you can see, we are still hopelessly deadlocked. It is evident that the company has no intention of dealing in good faith.

At this point the term "take-aways" first appeared in the union's bulletins (refering to demands by the company to take away benefits that the union had gained in previous negotiations), and the union had settled on mandatory overtime as the issue around which they would rally members. On October 27 one management issue was resolved—provisions for inverse seniority during temporary layoffs—but a few days later talks ended, and 35,000 workers went out on strike.

Only one meeting was held in November, while each side proclaimed in public that it would stand by its demands. The

4. *Fort Wayne Journal-Gazette,* August 10, 1979.
5. *Fort Wayne Journal-Gazette,* August 9, 1979.

company set up a toll-free hot line to present its positions to any who were interested and sent letters to striking employees, including a summary of their offer to the union. In the meantime the union rallied its members by reminding workers of the history of management abuse (in one case harkening back to the Haymarket Square massacre of 1886), emphasizing the "rights" of workers to bid freely for better jobs at work, and focusing on McCardell's salary and intentions (he was picked as the "goat" said one local leader).

When they met again on December 13, the company presented a new, additional, proposal for a four-day, ten-hour-per-day workweek in some plants. Meetings ended two days later. Around New Year's Day, the two lead bargainers met briefly at Midway Airport in Chicago, but nothing could be resolved. There was, as Marsh (1985, 216) reported, no rapport between the two men. During the holidays, union anger and frustration increased another notch. One plant guard said that, before Christmas, workers "all felt that the company's going to call it quits before the holiday and we're all going to make friends," but "after the holidays it was more of an attitude of 'we're going to get even with them.'"

In January IH began to face unexpected losses and cut the pay of 3,500 managers. By the end of the month the strike became the longest multiple-plant strike in UAW history and was, according to the *Chicago Tribune* (February 3, 1980), "rapidly becoming the bitterest." Worker anger focused on McCardell, who was arguing the company's position through the local media. When the two sides finally met again in early February, the company dropped its demand for mandatory overtime but introduced a new proposal for around-the-clock operations (seen by some as a backhanded way of achieving mandatory overtime). Chandler then wrote to workers to say that, with mandatory overtime dropped, the union was keeping workers on the streets for "unknown reasons." In the meantime, on the telephone hot line the company accused Pat Greathouse, the union's lead bargainer, of not meeting so that he could take a trip to Japan. Greathouse was "livid" over the remark, Chandler reported. In the next Negotiations Report put out by Local 98 in Indianapolis (February 13, 1980) IH was accused of trying to bargain through the press, they were called dishonest, and in response to their claim that the union's obstinacy was costing the average worker too much, the union countered "no price is too great to retain one's pride and self-respect." The union planned to confront McCardell directly at the company's annual stockholders' meeting on February 21 (they owned some shares of IH), but the company tried to keep them out by holding the meeting in a room with a limited capacity; the union sued and won an emergency order from the Federal District Court in Chicago requiring Harvester to move the meeting to a larger venue and open the meeting to all stockholders.

By early January some managers and board members began to question the company's strategy. One director said: "We began to let Archie know that the strike was costing us more than we thought it would, and the business wasn't going to get better as fast as he thought." The company's chief financial officer did analyses that showed the company losing more money than it could afford and suggested settling as soon as possible. "But," he said, "the problem we ran into, frankly, was that it was about four months into the strike [that] we made that decision [and] it took us about two months to end the strike." Some union leaders called the strike a "holy war," children were appearing on picket lines with signs saying "My Daddy Spends His Weekends with Me," and there were scattered violent incidents at plants around the country.

In March public reports[6] indicated that the mandatory overtime issue was settled but that seniority rules were still a problem and that a new "third major issue" was in the air: a demand
that IH would not interfere with the UAW if it tried to organize
new IH plants. On March 19 Greathouse brought a request to the
Harvester Council that the rank and file be allowed to ratify the
terms of the contract agreed to by that point while the bargaining committee ironed out the rest of the issues. The council
rejected the request but did give the bargaining committee the
power to decide when to send the contract to the rank and file
for ratification.[7] Final agreements on how to manage seniority
rights were negotiated locally over the next several weeks, and
negotiators returned to the main table on April 16. The next day
an agreement was reached, and each side declared victory.

Within the next two weeks, however, while the plants were
still restarting and employees were still being called back, layoffs
were announced. With the company getting financially weaker
every week, layoffs continued for another two years. IH would
never employ as many workers as it did before the strike and
would eventually have to sell off its major businesses—construction and farm equipment—to its former competitors. IH is now a
medium-sized truck manufacturer called Navistar. As one worker put it, "Everybody lost. Nobody won. Everybody bit off their
nose to spite their face."

After the strike was over, there was plenty of blame to spare.
Many workers felt just as bitter toward the union as they did
toward the company. One said: "They didn't want management
to have a say over anything. They strike just to show their
power. To me it was a nonsense strike." And McCardell was
accused by his own managers of making decisions based too
much on ego. Having lost so much already, neither the union

---

6. *Fort Wayne Journal-Gazette*, March 16, 1980.
7. *Fort Wayne Journal-Gazette*, March 20, 1980.

nor McCardell wanted to go back to tell their constituents that their efforts were for nought. One of the most telling criticisms was from a management negotiator who was astonished at McCardell's strategy of putting company bargainers (including himself) on local TV: "What arrogance to go on TV and try to convince not only employees but the local communities of your righteousness." McCardell's mistake, he said, was to naively believe that all he had to do was to "tell the people and they will come to the party." Such an approach might seem straightforward and rational. The results were not.

The Effects of Management's Approach to Bargaining

Much of the process of escalation and entrenchment that developed at IH could be attributed to the company's new approach to negotiations, the responses it engendered within the union, and the effect those reactions had on the union's leadership. With new personnel taking an unexpected approach, there was little trust between lead bargainers. By eliminating rituals that it saw as dysfunctional, the company eliminated the union leadership's means of internal control, affecting the union's ability both to respond to the company and to manage itself internally. We can see these dynamics by examining the reactions of different groups within the union to management's negotiators and the way in which they bargained.

Loss of Trust, Private Understanding, and Lead Bargainer Control

The union's top negotiators—full-time international staffers who were experienced negotiating professionals—were greatly concerned about the competence of their counterparts. Pat Greathouse, the union's lead bargainer, was alarmed that

Hayford initiated a new proposal for round-the-clock operations in the middle of bargaining, "He's proposing that four months into a strike! He has no concept of what goes on." About Chandler, he commented: "He would make a nice neighbor [but he] didn't know the shops or shop problems. He never tried to learn. All he was, really, was a transmission guy from the guys upstairs that were making raw pronouncements back down to the bargaining table." With these men in charge, the company was ill-informed, and its strategy poorly executed. As Art Shy, an administrative assistant to Greathouse, saw it:

> They offered us everything. They weren't trying any back-to-work movement, they weren't trying to bust the union. . . .They just felt that . . . they had to have [their demands]. But the most stupid thing was *telling* people, "Sure you can have all these things, but here's the things that we have to have."

He felt that Chandler was "lost, he had no knowledge of what even the conversations were about most of the time at the bargaining table." In the eyes of the union's top negotiators the company's bargaining strategists and lead bargainers were simply incapable of negotiating: They were not able to "talk intelligently" about their issues, did not know how to justify the changes that they requested, and did not know how to exchange ideas. Requisite expertise in the process and content of negotiations was not there, so they could not trust their opponents and could not count on them to manage the process in predictable and skillful ways.

Most frustrating to the union's lead bargainers was the loss of private means of communication. Horace Williams, another administrative assistant to Greathouse, worried that Chandler was not able to read the union accurately; he did not understand "Shy's determination or the leadership's determination, or the membership's determination. He had no idea." As another union official described it, "A lot of times . . . you know the other guy is catching what you're saying. You may not have to say it directly to him. Chandler didn't do that." Moreover, he added, Chandler was not clear about the company's position: "The things he would say would not tell you where he was really coming from." Even as a "transmission guy," according to this union official, "Greathouse was concerned because he wasn't sure that [Chandler] could carry our message to his own people and do it right." The UAW's lead bargainers could not trust Harvester's lead bargainers to know how to send or understand signals across the bargaining table.

To make matters worse, there were no sidebar meetings. Typically, said Williams, off-the-record meetings allowed each side to "feel out" the other's positions so that "there was no second guessing, no surprises. Everybody knew where they stood, their strengths and weaknesses." But Chandler refused to meet on the side. "We couldn't do that in these negotiations," Shy explained. "You couldn't do it. You couldn't meet with them. When we ended the strike with them, it was right at the bargaining table." The few old-hand negotiators on the company's team also noted the lack of interplay between Greathouse and Chandler; they did not, as was traditional, "talk positions through and find out where the hot buttons were and when the settlement time was." To their surprise, "Greathouse and Chandler never met one-on-one in the last month or two of the strike. The most it ever got to was, I think, four or five of us and four or five of them."

Lacking private means of communication and familiarity with the approach to bargaining that the company was using, the lead bargainers' ability to control negotiations through displays of expertise was weakened. They could not understand, interpret, nor predict management's actions. One local chairman who had looked to the lead bargainers for guidance said, "I saw Pat Greathouse and Art Shy and some of the guys that had been around just shaking their heads, and they were confused. I said, 'Geez, I'm in trouble.'" Greathouse and Shy were still in charge, but as negotiations progressed it was the local presidents, increasingly angry and militant, that took more control. At one point in the middle of the strike, Greathouse wanted to give the company some face-saving concessions to end the strike, but the bargaining councils, made up of local presidents and chairmen, refused even such token changes. And, when Greathouse met with the bargaining council on March 20 to suggest that they allow the rank and file to ratify what had been agreed upon at that point, the hard-liners were in control, and only 10 of the councils' 300 members voted with him.

Escalation of Public Conflict

While the lead bargainers were frustrated with the incompetence of their opponents, the lack of private communication, and their inability therefore to manage negotiations as they typically had, others on the bargaining team and in the union leadership became increasingly emotional and saw the negotiations in highly personalistic terms. One international union staffer who observed the negotiations said that the "attitude of Chandler and Mortonson pissed people off . . . pissed me off." As one local chairman put it:

> They were trying to take away a lot of things, and they didn't even put an economic package on the table. They were just looking to hold it out. They were just looking to prolong the strike, to beat up on us.

The company's approach was deemed "arrogant" by other local leaders. One of them said, "Any time you've got demands and you just take a hard stand, 'We're going to get these or else,' that to me is arrogant. There's no room for adjustment." Another local leader described the company's attitude:

I think there was an air about them, that they thought they knew more about things than a person like myself that doesn't have a college education. They felt that they were superior to us, so they wanted to put the screws to us. At least that's how I felt about it.

These local union leaders were quick to note differences in style that heightened the distinction between the two sides. One international staffer described how "one guy on their side came in wearing an ascot, . . . so after they left, some of the guys were putting the napkins on so they could have their little ascots on. It looked like some of these guys came out of the yacht club or something to meet with us." Such a mistake is rare among experienced bargainers who know the traditional roles and rituals of bargaining; usually these local leaders dealt with managers who could "cuss as good as we could."

The difference between these leaders and the top bargainers was that the local leaders saw the company's actions as intentionally malicious, not a result of inexperience. And they saw particular individuals leading the charge against them. "We thought it was Hayford and McCardell and Chandler. We felt after a while that they were just trying to kill us, destroy us," explained one local leader. In an unusual expression of vindictiveness, another local leader commented that, when Warren Mortonson had a heart attack a short way into the strike, "Nothing did more to lift our spirits. No sympathy. Nothing. It was a bitter one."

The rank and file, having only the reports from their leaders and what they knew from the press, focused all their hatred on Archie McCardell and developed a caricatured view of him that included many dubious facts. Here are some samples:

Look what Archie did to Xerox—bankrupted 'em. Archie wanted to do one thing, bust the union. He didn't care how he did it. The guys down here are like spit on his shoes.

There's a quote that he says he wants to break the union. That's a fact. He was so against the union and American workers. I read about it in the paper.

I could never find the purported article in which McCardell said that he would break the union, but he was known, among managers as well as union officials, to be loose with the press. Even if McCardell did not say so directly, workers inferred his intentions from the strategy he chose. A worker argued:

[I knew] that Archie McCardell wanted to break the union . . . by the fact that he was breaking time-honored traditions of the way we did our negotiating. He was going to do something different that was never done before, so the only way I could interpret it is "break the union . . . going to teach us a lesson."

The company's demands—especially mandatory overtime—did not make sense to union members, so they thought the company's only purpose was to intentionally and for no good reason to put workers out "on the streets": "The company threw everything at us, knowing we couldn't accept it. They just wanted to get us out of production," said another worker. Anger built up to the point where some were willing to "irrationally" risk their livelihoods to beat the company.

Once there was this much anger among the rank and file, the leadership had few options. According to an International staffer, "We would have got killed if we would have brought back any form of mandatory overtime." Greathouse explained that the resistance that had built up "certainly made it impossible to give into [McCardell's] demands because that was a wall that was built up from day one." He could not compromise, even on minor issues. He explained:

I recognized the importance of face saving in these things. . . . .By March, it was obvious . . . that they were in real trouble, employmentwise, and I was trying, pushing hard, to work out a settlement. And then at that meeting of the Council on the 19th of March . . . I suggested, "Why don't we say that if they settle everything, one that we'd give them was [to eliminate the piece-worker's right to go home if his job had run out]." I said, "Nobody's going to use it anymore. Why don't we give them that one." [They said], "No way. We're not going to give them anything."

The company's old-hand negotiators felt pushed aside, the union's lead bargainers were made powerless, and the process was one of pure clash between the two sides. Traditionally the drama of conflict would have been mitigated by backstage signaling and sidebar discussions. Those rituals, and the pragmatic discussion which they allowed, were absent at IH in 1979.

Ignoring Roles and Rituals

The structure of interaction that developed in these negotiations is displayed in figure 8.1. The process changes implemented by McCardell and Chandler eliminated the traditional mechanisms for cross-table communication: signaling, and sidebar discussions. As a result there was no means for private understanding between opposing bargainers, so that misperceptions developed and there was no way to make appropriate adjustments. These

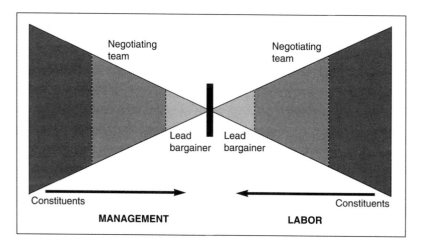

Figure 8.1
Interaction pattern at International Harvester

changes also made it harder for the union's lead bargainers to act like experts, be more "in the know" than others, and shape the team's interpretation of reality. Control shifted away from the lead bargainers and into the hands of local leaders and the rank and file. What was left was a direct confrontation between the two constituencies—McCardell and the workers.

I do not mean to claim that Harvester's violation of the traditional roles and rituals of labor negotiations caused the strike at IH. I do mean to say that the frustration of the union's lead bargainers, the related shift of control away from the lead bargainers, and the high level of anger among workers and local leaders were due to the fact that traditional roles and rituals were unilaterally ignored. Simply ignoring roles and rituals, it appears, is a highly risky strategy for changing negotiations. It applies a blunt instrument to a complex system, and the results are, at best, unpredictable. Moreover traditional expectations are difficult to escape if an alternative approach is not explicitly agreed upon; as long as established expectations and the social conditions that generated them persist, the opponent will continue to depend on and use the traditional rituals, and interpret deviations from them as indications of incompetence, a lack of integrity, or a lack of goodwill.

9   Reshaping Roles and Rituals: Midwestern University

At Midwestern University the administration and its faculty union, the American Faculty Union (AFU), talked about their dissatisfaction with the traditional rituals of bargaining and agreed to try something new. They put their negotiators through joint training in a process called "mutual gains bargaining" (MGB). At the end of training the two sides developed a set of "ground rules" which they tried to follow throughout most of their negotiations. What is distinctive about the change that occurred at Midwestern is that, compared to the IH case, both labor and management shared in the decision to change the process, and compared to the NBP negotiations, the changes that were made were done publicly and with the agreement of constituents. They consciously tried to reshape the traditional roles and rituals of labor negotiations. They engaged all of the parties involved—including constituents, lead bargainers, and team members—in an open discussion about the process and tried to *change the expectations* that these parties place on each other.

Many of the negotiators were pleased with the new process and the results it produced: Negotiations were less acrimonious than ever before, there were some innovative agreements, and they reached settlement early. Nonetheless, they had to repeatedly face traditional expectations among some constituents and deal with the ambiguity of using a new and unfamiliar approach. And, toward the end of negotiations the process became very traditional. They faced these difficulties, even though the situation that they started with was in many ways ideal for generating change: There was general dissatisfaction with the traditional process, negotiators were chosen who were not negotiating pros and who were predisposed to labor-management cooperation, administration negotiators were line managers not staff, and both the university and the union were free from outside control. In other cases where MGB was tried, under less auspicious circumstances, the process was simply dropped. Two cases of this type are discussed in chapter 10.

The Ideas of Mutual Gains Bargaining

Mutual gains bargaining is an approach to negotiations that various authors and consultants have called "win-win," "principled," or "integrative" bargaining.[1] It is based on the notion that it is not always necessary to take from the other to get more for oneself.[2] If negotiators can avoid some of the behaviors typical of traditional bargaining, they can find creative solutions that help both sides. The two main behaviors that MGB is designed to change are (1) sticking rigidly to a given set of ideas or proposals and (2) acting out of emotion and anger rather than analysis.

The first step in MGB is to present to the opponent, not proposals for solving problems, but the problems themselves. Negotiators must distinguish between their underlying "inter-

---

1. Several recent authors in this tradition include Fisher and Ury (1981), Susskind and Cruikshank (1987), and Lax and Sebenius (1986). In this section I draw primarily from Fisher and Ury, unless otherwise specified.

2. In economic parlance the proposition is that negotiations can be "positive sum" rather than "zero sum," or, to put it another way, that negotiators can take actions that move them closer to the Pareto frontier, or push out the Pareto frontier, rather than just redistributing a given amount of utility.

ests" and particular "positions" for addressing those interests. Second, once interests are understood, negotiators should take the time to create and explore as many different options as possible for meeting those interests. This increases the chance that they will find better solutions, and ones that both sides can accept.

The distinction between interests and positions is illustrated in a story told by Mary Parker Follett (1942), who introduced the idea of "integrative" conflict resolution in the 1930s. A friend of Follett's wanted to sail to Europe but could not afford the trip. Follett tried to help her distraught friend by encouraging her to think about what it was she really wanted. In Follett's conceptual terms, she helped her friend to break the "whole" into its "constituent parts." Going to Europe could mean many different things, including "a sea voyage, seeing beautiful places, [or] meeting new people" (p. 41). For her friend, Follett found out, going to Europe was desirable primarily because it involved meeting people. Once she realized that, her friend was able to find an alternative for the summer that met her true desires: She taught at a summer school where she would meet an interesting group of students. According to Follett, "This was not a substitution for her wish, it was her *real* wish" (p. 42). By focusing on her underlying interests rather then remaining stuck on her commitment to a particular position (going to Europe), Follett's friend was able to achieve her true goals despite financial constraints. The difficulty of this approach is being very clear about what you really want, and avoiding premature commitment to one way of achieving those wants. It takes a concerned effort not to become committed, early in negotiations, to the most obvious or prominent ideas.

The other behavior that MGB is designed to change is the tendency to become committed to courses of actions out of anger, pride, or feelings of personal antipathy toward opposing negotiators. Fisher and Ury (1981) admonish negotiators to "separate

- Separate the people from the problems
- Focus on interests, not positions
- Invent options for mutual gain
- Insist on using objective criteria

Figure 9.1
Major points of *Getting to Yes*

the people from the problems" and encourage negotiators to look for "objective standards" for evaluating ideas. This takes some of the emotion away from negotiations and puts the focus on analysis rather than either anger or power. Fisher and Ury's main prescriptions are listed in figure 9.1.

Within MGB, each side is encouraged to tell the other side its interests and engage in an open discussion of ideas for satisfying those interests. This does not mean being nice to the opponent but rather being clear about what you want. As Follett explained:

A friend of mine said to me, "Open-mindedness is the whole thing, isn't it?" No, it isn't; it needs just as great a respect for your own view as for that of others, and a firm upholding of it until you are convinced. Mushy people are not more good at this than stubborn people. (p. 48)

An integrative approach, she explained, discourages parties from trying to dominate each other, but it also discourages them from compromising—if compromising means accepting a deal that does not meet your interests.

Midwestern University

In 1989 the administration and the faculty union at Midwestern University decided to try MGB. The previous round of negotiations had been quite difficult: The bitter negotiations had dragged on for eight months.[3] Most agreed that the administration's lead bargainer had been extremely contentious in his approach. Dissatisfaction with the negotiation process became apparent as the 1989 round drew near; few wanted to negotiate if it meant being subjected to the same kind of antagonism experienced last time. Therefore the union and administration were looking for an alternative approach to negotiations. Through some contacts with faculty at the Harvard Program on Negotiation, they learned of the Department of Labor project on MGB and agreed to be one of three test sites in return for free training.

Initially the union did not want to try using MGB. Although a new board had been elected that wanted a more cooperative approach to bargaining, there was still a great deal of resistance from the "loony left" (a phrase used by the union and administration alike). Before the union could agree to MGB training, it debated the issue. In the fall of 1988, in an open forum, a trainer from the Program on Negotiation argued for the use of MGB, while a union representative from another school argued against it. Eventually union members decided to allow their negotiators to use MGB but insisted that if the process did not result in an agreement by the beginning of summer (three months before the contract was to expire), they should revert to traditional negotiations.

Meanwhile, on both sides, team members were chosen who had an interest in MGB. On the union's side, the lead negotiator accepted the job under the condition that negotiations be non-confrontational. He put together a team of moderates, a difficult task since moderates were usually not very active in the union. On the administration's side, the lead bargainer was a former president of the AFU and the dean of one of the university's colleges. The people on his team were also deans or associate deans. Except for the administration's contract administrator, the

---

3. In a survey of union leaders and administrators, neither side felt that the other understood its situation in those negotiations.

university team was made up of line managers rather than staff. As a result the people at the table had direct knowledge about most of the workings of the university. On both sides of the table, only two of the fourteen negotiators had ever been in negotiations before (the staff administrators on each side), so the group carried few preset notions of how bargaining should be conducted.

Overall relations between faculty and the administration at the university were somewhat strained as negotiations began. The president of the university had been an academic in a business school earlier in his career, but came to his position at Midwestern from a job in industry. Some faculty members saw him as a businessman who was not a scholarly leader. To make matters worse, earlier in his career, he had written an article in which he commented that deception was one way to approach unions. In addition there were a number of other problems at the school: a recent sex-discrimination lawsuit over tenure had been won by the faculty member, the faculty senate was perceived as an ossified institution, and the university was only weakly unified—each of its many schools operated as almost independent entities. Although the administration and the union were willing to approach negotiations with a positive attitude in 1989, relations between the two sides were generally strained.

Training

A month prior to the start of bargaining, negotiators at Midwestern received two days of training. On the first day, training included members of the union's board of directors and bargaining council (as well as their eight negotiators) and most of the school's top administrators (as well as their eight negotiators). The trainer explained the ideas of MGB and gave everyone a chance to use the ideas in an hour-long one-on-one simulation of negotiations to familiarize them with the basic ideas of MGB and help them to see its benefits.

During a second day of training, the negotiators engaged in an extensive simulation of labor negotiations that included many issues and several different parties on each side. For this simulation administrators played the role of union negotiators, and union negotiators played the role of management. This was designed to help each side see the other's point of view. At the end of the simulation they met to discuss their reactions.

These negotiators were excited by the basic ideas of MGB: They seemed to like the fact that the process was guided by a theory (one negotiator was interested in exploring the similarities between MGB and transactional analysis in psychology), and they respected the trainer and his credentials. Given their overall lack of bargaining experience, most did not have old habits to overcome. Although they made a sincere and concerted effort to use the process in the simulation, they found translating the ideas of MGB into action difficult. Most important, while the distinction between interests and positions seemed clear in the lectures, it seemed less clear in practice.

The simulation was taken seriously, but it was also a time for negotiators to get to know each other, acknowledge their differences, and laugh about those differences. During one simulation a union representative, playing the role of a management negotiator, explained that his company's subcontracting request was "a matter of management rights." An administration negotiator, stepping momentarily out of his union role, exclaimed happily upon hearing the words "management rights," "It's in their vocabulary!" Another union representative quickly stepped out of his character and joked in response, "We've also heard of the divine right of kings!"

Implementing MGB: Getting Ready

A few weeks after these two days of training, the teams got together to write up their own rules for bargaining (see figure

---

Reporting and accountability to the constituents

- Define second table so that authority and relationships are understood.
- Share explicit strategies for dealing with these constituencies.
- Insist that constituents develop options and not positions.
- Issue reports (perhaps joint) to our constituents; tone of presentation must be consistent on both sides.
- AFU Newsletter will include, throughout the process, a "from the table" column to keep the bargaining unit informed of the issues; will discuss options and interests being explored at the table.
- Faculty Senate reports will be based upon the constituents' reports.

Press relations

- Seek to manage for benefit of communication to the community (MU and beyond) but will not black out.
- Issue joint press release, as necessary, tied to the constituent reports; Bob Foot will draft these press releases and submit for joint team review.
- Both sides will have one official spokesperson for the press; other press contact will be forbidden.

Negotiating ground rules

- Establish internal procedures for team meetings and agenda setting.
- Set agenda for each subsequent meeting before adjournment.
- Establish time limits for caucuses.
- Establish a commonly agreed upon set of demographics about the bargaining unit (size, average age, salary ranges, etc.). This will be done jointly with help of Roy Seth.
- Establish a precise mechanism for joint investigation of data, including access to and use of expert presentations.
- Explicitly separate invention from commitment and creation from analysis.
- Explicitly avoid closure on single issues
    trade options
    link issues
    develop packages
- Attorneys for the AFU and administration may be consulted as appropriate, but will be permitted to attend sessions only by mutual consent and only as silent observers, unless joint agreement otherwise.
- Facilitators, including Federal Mediation and Conciliation Service, will be consulted as needed by mutual agreement.
- Subcommittees of team members may be used to generate ideas and develop options about specific topics; okay to add other people outside the teams to these subcommittees.

These ground rules may always be modified by joint agreement.

Figure 9.2
Midwestern University's draft ground rules

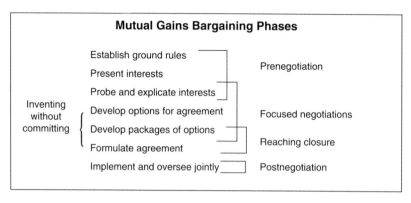

Figure 9.3
Midwestern University's phase model of MGB

9.2) and develop their own model for the process (see figure 9.3). They emphasized areas they saw as most critical, included procedures that addressed their particular needs, and described the process in their own words. The fact that they were using a new bargaining process was widely publicized in the school newspaper and in the union's bargaining reports to its members. Negotiators at Midwestern were fully and explicitly committed to a different process of bargaining and would try to implement, as best they could, the ideas and techniques that they had just learned.

After the ground rules were written, each side spent the last weeks before negotiations creating a description of their interests in each topic area. Within the union, this involved meetings of the negotiating team, various subcommittees, the board of directors for the union, and the union's bargaining council (a group of about 40 union members who were interested in helping set guidelines for the negotiations). In one of its "Reports from the Table," the union explained how it distinguished between interests and positions and its view of the importance of doing so:

Setting forth and probing essential interests provides the basis for suggesting options for achieving desirable ends later in the process. First we say what kind of university and faculty we see as ideal, then we spell out how to get there. This is quite different from traditional bargaining where each side says what it wants, but fails to tell the other side exactly why it wants it or how it will further mutual interests to get it. We assume, after looking at interest statements, that there will be overlap between what the faculty and the Board of Trustee's desire.

In substantive terms, the issues to be covered in the negotiations included faculty development, benefits, salary, and governance. Based on a survey of all participants during the first day of training, both sides were most concerned about benefits, with salaries following close behind. These two issues would provide the greatest challenge for negotiators, and created the greatest amount of conflict.

The First Days: Discussing Interests

Joint meetings began on April 10. Without a clear ritual to follow, negotiators were unsure what would happen. In the union caucus prior to the joint meeting, one negotiator asked the group, "Who should talk?" and another asked, "Can anyone jump in?" The one experienced negotiator, the union's staff administrator, cautioned them not to "look confused" and to caucus if needed. She was familiar with the traditional rituals of bargaining and concerned that they look unified and in control. The lead bargainer countered that, with MGB, they should not have to caucus; there was no way that talking openly about interests could hurt them.

When negotiations began, everyone worked hard to organize his or her comments according to the MGB model and focus on interests rather than positions. When one union negotiator found himself making a specific suggestion, he stopped himself and said, "No, that's getting into 'options.' Forget that." Later, an administration negotiator said, "I understand your position," which engendered an emphatic "Interest!" on the part of a union negotiator. The administrator then smiled, slapped his hand, and apologized. They also created a new language of their own. In one example, a union negotiator expressed dissatisfaction with a formula for determining summer salaries, saying that it should be 33.3% of the regular salary, not 30%. An administrator suggested, "Shouldn't we leave it at the interest level?" Another union negotiator responded, "We're not sure exactly what we want. Let's explore." They decided to create a new word, "problem," to avoid the linguistic roadblock they were feeling. They were trying to perform for each other, but what they wanted to convey was the strength of their effort to use MGB, not their loyalty to teammates or opposition to the other side.

At the same time it became apparent that each side had a different understanding of what interests were and was frustrated that the other side was not discussing them properly. Management interests, such as its stated desire for "excellence," were seen as too vague by the union. In the meantime the union responded to the administration's very broad interest statements by assuming that interests were code words for what the administration really wanted: When the administration talked about "excellence," the union responded, "Oh, you mean the `M' word [i.e., merit pay]?" They were still expecting traditional signals. The next day, an administration negotiator argued that management did *not* have a position behind its interests, as the union had implied. A union negotiator responded, "We don't either, but our second table[4] does!" This comment reminded everyone that they were still constrained to some degree by their traditional roles as representatives. Meanwhile the administration saw the union's interests (e.g., "faculty salaries at the two comprehensive universities in the state should be equal") as "positions, not interests." It interpreted the union's presentation of its interests as "classic union behavior." The next day a union negotiator

---

4. They used the term "second table" to refer to constituents. The term comes from the observation that each team negotiated with constituents as well as opponents: they have a "second" bargaining table.

responded to these sentiments with an emphatic declaration, "These *are* interests, not positions."

In the first week negotiators were creating a new process. They had a theory around which to construct this new process but needed to discover how to behave in action: They had to develop new bargaining rituals, a new vocabulary, and new roles for themselves. There was no well-understood ritual and no clear sense of lead bargainer control (the lead bargainers knew the process no better than anyone else). Initially each side's members thought the other was incompetent: Their side was doing MGB right, while the other side was not.

Over the next several days, they settled down and adjusted to each other and the new process. After initially blaming the union for presenting positions rather than interests, the administration's lead bargainer tried to help by rewriting those positions in a form that seemed more focused on interests. Then, after initially (and automatically) labeling this document "confidential," the administration's lead bargainer ripped off the part of the document with "confidential" stamped on it and gave the document to the union when they met. Negotiators sat intermingled, rather than opposite each other at the bargaining table, and neither side stopped to caucus during joint meetings. Most negotiators participated actively in the process: They helped describe and clarify their side's interests, questioned each other, and recorded issues on the flip chart. And they directed as many questions toward teammates as toward opponents. None of the rituals of opposition, representation, or control were performed. In their report from the table, the AFU commented, "In the three joint meetings during the first two weeks, the two teams have begun to respect each other's integrity." There was "occasional friction," he added, "but it was resolved quickly so as not to leave scars." Even for external audiences, displays of antagonism were eliminated.

The "Great Budget Shoot-out"

The first major roadblock the negotiators faced was the "great budget shoot-out," as it was called by negotiators, scheduled for the second week of negotiations. For negotiators to evaluate each other's proposals using objective criteria, as MGB said they should, they needed some objective data. Most important, they needed to develop a common understanding of the financial condition of the university. Therefore the union hired an outside analyst, John March, to report on the university's finances at a joint meeting that included the university's financial officer. In case of discrepancies, a neutral consultant was hired to assess the accuracy of the two views.

March reported that the university was in excellent financial shape, while the university's financial officer argued that there was growth in the school's "restricted" funds,[5] but not in its "general" funds, and that it would be inappropriate to aggregate those funds for the purpose of assessing the university's financial condition. The neutral consultant, who was from an accounting firm, said that both sides were right to a certain degree: The university was not in great financial shape, but it was exactly where a university of this type should be. There were sound reasons to keep some units of the university financially separate from each other, but many of those divisions were a matter of choice—these were managerial decisions that might or might not be operationally sound. To the great frustration of all, these experts could not agree on the financial status of the university. Finding the "truth," it seemed, would require someone to analyze each of the hundreds of individual accounting decisions that were part of the budget; neither side wanted to get dragged

---

5. The reason for being restricted varied. Some funds were restricted because it was money paid *through* the university for services provided by semiautonomous units such as the blood center or the medical school's practice plans.

into this financial quagmire. Any hopes for evaluating salary options objectively were dashed.

The event also created unexpected conflicts. The second half of the shoot-out was an open meeting of administrators and faculty intended to inform them about the results of the budget analysis. While negotiators had come to know and trust each other, this was not the case among constituents: Some of the more radical faculty members directly challenged the administration in a very confrontational way during the meeting, and union negotiators became upset at what they saw as rude and disrespectful "snickering" and "eye rolling" on the part of the deans who were not on the negotiating team. In one critical incident a union negotiator tried to get the neutral consultant to answer one important, specific question: Based on his assessment, the negotiator asked, would it be possible for the administration to "salt away" $10 million or $15 million for a new football stadium? The president, indignant that someone asked the neutral a question that he himself had answered moments before, proclaimed, "You are calling me a liar!" He stood up and stormed out of the room.

The following day both sides expressed frustration with their constituents and their inability to figure out the university's finances. But there was a positive side: One administrator pointed out that the "remarkable amount of openness" displayed by the finance officer was "something that you would never see in traditional bargaining." Even though there was still a great deal of confusion about the financial health of the university, and lingering suspicions about hidden funds, the union learned that administrators were also confused about the budget and felt that the administration's negotiators were not purposely misleading them. One union negotiator pointed out that "in traditional bargaining, you would have a report in the newspaper about the president" in order to build up union solidarity and anger. Nothing like that occurred this time.

The next day someone brought in a bottle of champagne, explaining, "We need one good experience together" after the budget shoot-out. They toasted to getting a good agreement and finishing the MGB process. The bargainers were able to get past this personal confrontation but were left wary of intrusions by their constituents and frustrated with their inability to develop objective criteria for evaluating financial proposals.

Developing Options

As negotiators moved to the next stage of the MGB process—developing a list of possible agreements or options—they once again confronted differences of opinion about how to proceed. No one quite knew how this stage of negotiations should work: Were they supposed to talk about options for the whole package, or just individual issues? How many options should they generate? Were options the same as offers? Each side had different answers to these questions and different worries about what might go wrong. For several weeks, a consistent side issue in the negotiations was how they would go about developing options.

As the negotiators began to develop new ideas, the union's lead bargainer mentioned some of them during board meetings; he was concerned about the board's responses to the new ideas and wanted to keep the members informed. The administration's lead bargainer, hearing about these concerns, countered that if constituents were involved, they would be critical of new ideas: "You can't invent in an atmosphere of criticism." He also worried that constituents would force negotiators to commit themselves to particular options.

The union's lead bargainer also expressed a desire to break into subcommittees. That way, he suggested, they could quickly arrive at a few viable options and would not all have to waste time learning about the intricate details of the medical college (its particular complexities had confused everyone). Administrators, by contrast, wanted all the negotiators to continue to work together to develop as many options as possible. They worried that subcommittees might become committed to certain options too early, would not generate as many options, and would get too far ahead of the rest of the negotiators. Moreover the hard-earned sense of shared purpose and momentum in the larger group would be lost.

They decided to stay together, but agreed that each side should come to the table with two options for each subject area and explain how these options met both side's interests. They would be careful to avoid either criticizing these ideas or becoming committed to them. One negotiator suggested, "Give Don and Len a red flag, and if it looks like we're coming to a position, they start waving and hollering." As one administrator put it, they seemed to be agreeing to have a "private, creative phase" during which "we wouldn't say a whole lot to our constituencies." She asked, "Are we collectively O.K. to kind of close the door for two weeks and say that 'now this group is getting down to business—we'll talk to you later'?" The union agreed, with the caveat that it still had to talk to its constituents in several scheduled meetings the next day and tell them that negotiations were moving into a confidential stage. An administrator joked, "Then they can become as paranoid about you as they are about us!" The ground rules that were agreed upon are shown in figure 9.4.

---

1. No discussion beyond the table until [we] mutually agree to release [information].
2. No option is too outrageous.
3. Avoid closure on single issues.
4. Free to invent without criticism; probing link between interest and options is desirable.
5. Criticism and revision follow the invention stage.
6. Need minimum of two options per interest category. (All options come in pairs.)

Figure 9.4
Ground rules for discussing options

During this creative stage many new ideas were generated. In response to the university's interest in encouraging more effort among senior faculty, one union member brought up the idea of a "phase" compensation plan that would include new categories within the full-professor ranks—this would encourage effort among senior faculty by putting more money in the pockets of those who were more productive. An administrator suggested that if faculty members could find ways to save the university money during the upcoming three years, that money would go into a pool that would be used to add another 2% to their salary increases. In the insurance area, they talked about every possible health care option. During this time they helped each other search for new solutions to each other's problems and tried to understand and explore every idea that was brought to the table—even ones that they knew would likely be rejected by constituents on one side or the other.

They did, however, discover some limits to brainstorming. Early discussion had convinced the administration that the problems at the medical school were so unique that they had to be dealt with separately. Therefore, when the options stage began, they suggested that the group first decide how to deal with the medical school. The administration's lead bargainer presented several "threshold" options, including having a separate section of the contract deal exclusively with the medical school, making it into a separate bargaining unit, or even decertifying it. Although some in the union had been forewarned about this idea, others on the union team responded with shock and anger. They all learned that brainstorming had some limits.

They also faced external constraints on brainstorming. Members of the union's bargaining council became irate when they heard about the "phase" idea for salary. They were upset about the content of the idea, but also about the fact that ideas were being discussed that they had not authorized. After they had done so much work to figure out what the membership wanted, some on the council argued, what right did the team have to act as independent agents? Role expectations for negotiators to act strictly as their representatives persisted. And they did not believe that it was possible for their negotiators to discuss ideas without becoming committed to them. One council member argued, "Once you put that corpse on the table, it will be impossible to push off." When the negotiators met the next day, one union negotiator explained the problem: "We've tried to say that options are options, and 90% of them just fall dead and never see more than the five minutes they're up on the blackboard. But I don't know what [constituents'] level of understanding is—whether they have internalized the message or whether they're still thinking of the old ways of doing things." On both sides, when new ideas reached constituents, they were often rejected without consideration; negotiators rarely had a chance to explain all of the factors that they had considered. Negotiators on both sides often sat silently as their weeks of work were summarily tossed out by the people to whom they reported.

Internal Success

Among themselves, negotiators at Midwestern managed to create an atmosphere of cooperation and exploration. Conflicts never remained personal. A day after an angry confrontation over faculty leaves, the union negotiator who had yelled at an administrator brought her a chair, saying, "This is the least I can do after what I put [you] through. It is called 'penance'." Each person on the team came to be seen as an individual with his or her own peculiarities, strengths, and flaws. One union negotiator was known for continually offering wild ideas, complete with elaborate documentation and flow charts. One day, when he had been mostly quiet, he announced proudly, "I have an idea!" The union's lead bargainer, with all watching, bowed his head, crossed himself as if praying, and everybody laughed. Halfway through negotiations, an administrator explained that she had "developed a certain confidence in our ability to come together and solve problems. We have demonstrated over and over again that rumors can float, misinformation can float, confrontations can occur, and we are able to figure out what to do about it and decide what we're going to do next."

The strength of relationships between the two sides can be seen in images created through network analysis. Four times during the negotiations (just prior to the start of negotiations, three weeks into negotiations, six weeks into negotiations, and the final week of negotiations), negotiators on both sides filled out survey questions asking whom they trusted. The pattern of responses for each period is displayed in figure 9.5. Management negotiators are represented on these diagrams by points M1–M8, while union negotiators are represented by points U1–U8. If a negotiator indicated that he or she trusted another negotiator, a line is drawn between those points. If each negotiator chose the other, the line has arrows on both ends. If one person chose the other, the arrow points only in that direction. People are located on the diagram according to their team and whether they were lead bargainers. Management negotiators are on the left side of the diagram, while union negotiators are on the right. The four negotiators with greatest formal responsibility for the negotiations—the lead bargainers and the labor relations administrators for each side—are located in the center while their teammates are located in a semicircle behind them.

As figure 9.5 shows, when negotiations began, there was only one trust tie between the two sides. As negotiations proceeded, trust increased so that by the middle of negotiations (time 3), there were several trust ties between the two sides and even

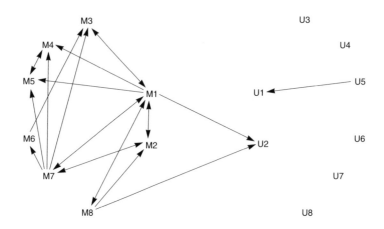

Management negotiators   **Union negotiators**

a. Trust ties, prior to negotiations (time 1)

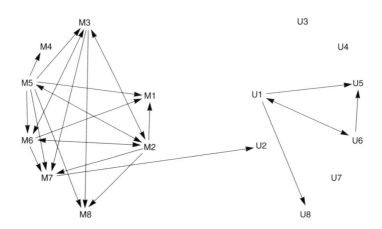

Management negotiators   **Union negotiators**

b. Trust ties, six weeks into negotiations (time 2)

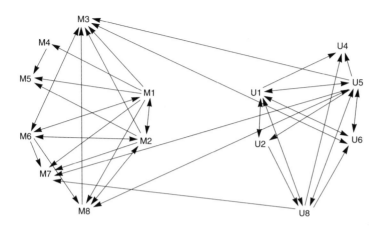

Management negotiators   **Union negotiators**

c. Trust ties, nine weeks into negotiations (time 3)

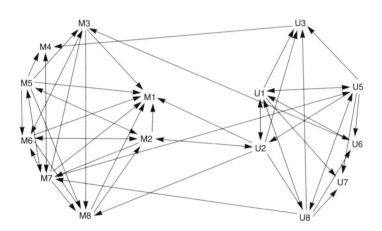

Management negotiators   **Union negotiators**

d. Trust ties, at end of negotiations (time 4)

Figure 9.5
Midwestern University's trust networks. (These images were created with
KrackPlot, Krackhardt, Lundberg, and O'Rourke 1993.)

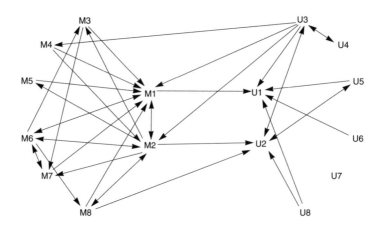

Management negotiators   **Union negotiators**

a. Advice ties, six weeks into negotiations (time 2)

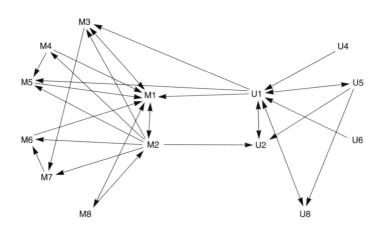

Management negotiators   **Union negotiators**

b. Advice ties, nine weeks into negotiations (time 3)

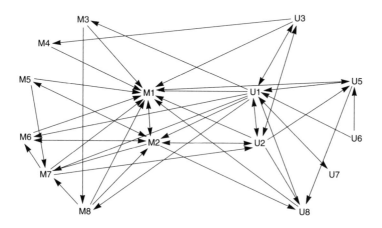

Management negotiators   **Union negotiators**

c. Advice ties, at end of negotiations (time 4)

Figure 9.6
Midwestern University's advice networks. (These images were created with
KrackPlot, Krackhardt, Lundberg, and O'Rourke 1993.)

more in the final days of negotiations (time 4). The kind of oppositional structure that is expected in labor negotiations broke
down in this case by the time negotiations were finished.

Negotiators were also asked, on the three surveys that
occurred after negotiations were underway, to indicate which
negotiators they could ask for advice about negotiations, if needed. The pattern of responses for each period is displayed in figure 9.6. As with the network images of trust, if each negotiator
chose the other, the line has arrows on both ends. If one person
chose the other, the arrow points only in that direction. These
images show a dense network of advice ties both within and
across the teams, especially at the end of negotiations (time 4),
indicating that leadership was shared. Taken together, figures 9.5
and 9.6 show that negotiators at Midwestern were able to escape
the kind of oppositional roles and strict leadership control that is
part of the traditional negotiation process.

External Constraints

At the same time negotiators learned that they still faced significant external constraints.

Constituents
Constituents had authorized the negotiators to use MGB, and some were given training in the process, but they were not part of the learning, growing, and testing of the process that the negotiators experienced. Only the negotiators internalized their understanding of MGB and came to truly believe in this process. While negotiators learned to distinguish interests and positions, constituents still thought in terms of positions. While negotiators understood that options were just possibilities, constituents had a hard time accepting that. While negotiators wanted to create an atmosphere of creativity, constituents were not completely comfortable letting their negotiators operate unfettered. They knew and accepted that MGB was being used but still had some expectations about how their negotiators should behave and held on to specific goals and objectives. The union rejected an administration request early in negotiations to put out a statement of common interests, saying, "It makes us look like we're selling out—[our constituents] don't want us to sell out until the last day."

Early in negotiations, constituents were less of a problem for the administration than for the union; for them, goals were more clearly defined, the administration had worked for years to develop its plan for negotiations, and there were fewer subgroups to deal with. At this point administrators were frustrated with the union team's seeming inability to act on its own, and were not fully sympathetic to its constraints. Later, however, as its constituents became more active and it faced many of the same constraints, it suddenly gained a great deal of sympathy for the union negotiators' constituent pressures.

In addition to getting ahead of constituents in process and ideas, negotiators forged bonds of trust between themselves, while there was still a "we–they" mentality among many of their constituents. Negotiators came to know and trust each other as individuals, but to many administrators, the union was still the enemy, and to many of the union's "loony left," the administration could do no good.

Finances

There were many areas where negotiators could be creative, but salary seemed not to be one of them. The university had a budget, which greatly constrained its options. Even the administration's negotiators were frustrated with the lack of space for maneuvering and with the sense that finances were inherently positional. During the great budget shoot-out, the financial officer revealed that the university budgeted for a 5.5% increase in faculty compensation. In their caucus administrators discussed their sense that a position had already been established for them. One negotiator later asked the lead bargainer: "What *are* our marching orders? Can we go past 5.5%?" He responded: "We have to generate options and take it back to our budget people. The president has not said, 'This is what you will do.' But should we stick to the budget? Yes, that's common sense." When salary options were presented later, each side was indignant that the other had not taken into consideration the interests and information that had been provided. An administration negotiator was shocked at the union's presentation of an option of 9% increase in salary, "Didn't they hear us?" And the union was angry that the administration did not take the union's financial analysis into consideration when it offered only a 2% wage increase (with some added money for merit increases over 2% for some faculty).

Time

When brainstorming succeeded, more ideas were brought up, requiring more time for discussion and analysis. Negotiators realized that they were already halfway through negotiations and that there was no end in sight to the work that had to be done. They were still working together as a whole, afraid to break their momentum by moving into subcommittees, and avoided bringing in outside topic experts since they would not understand the MGB process. On May 5 the MGB trainer visited the university and suggested that the only way to finish in time was to divide the work and assign different pieces to subcommittees. This advice was accepted, and subcommittee meetings began immediately. In the subcommittees negotiators studied existing options, generated additional ones, and began to form tentative agreements. During May most of the bargaining occurred in subcommittees. But again, each new idea created new demands for analysis, often by outside parties who could not provide quick reports.

Meanwhile the end of negotiations drew closer. Since many faculty left for the summer, a general meeting of the union was scheduled for June 8. At that time they would announce either that an agreement had been reached or that the MGB process had not worked, creating a concrete deadline for the negotiators.

Reverting to Traditional Bargaining

During most of negotiations, main-table discussions were never interrupted by caucus meetings—if people had problems, they discussed them openly. On May 24, with the newly created deadline approaching, the union called its first caucus. Shortly after that, most of the negotiating was done in small meetings between the top negotiators, and constituent leaders became more involved. At the trainer's suggestion, several constituents were brought to the main-table meetings. The internal cohesion that had developed among negotiators was placed under great strain. The university's budget was still not clear, nor was the actual amount of salary increase being offered.[6] The union's board and bargaining council were giving the bargaining team different directions. It seemed as if negotiations might collapse.

At this final stage, negotiations became very traditional. Innovative ideas that were developed through the MGB process (e.g., a formal clarification of the medical school's obligation to tenured faculty) were used as "chips" to be traded for higher salary increases, and the MGB process itself was turned into a chip. On the last day, just when negotiations were about to collapse, the president decided to meet the union's demand for across-the-board increases by eliminating merit pay. He came back with an offer of "6%, 5%, 5%, no merit pay, with the medical college package."

The union got the base wages it needed, and it maintained a no-premium indemnity option for health care; the administration stayed within its budget, placed a cap on its health care costs, and achieved language that defined for the first time its salary obligations to tenured medical school faculty in case their grant and practice incomes declined. There was a contingent of faculty members who were upset by the changes in the health plan, and some deans were upset by the loss of merit pay. Yet many creative ideas were generated during negotiations, a few survived, and the agreement was ratified by an overwhelming majority of the faculty and accepted by the board of trustees.

---

6. The two sides had difficulty translating percentages into flat amounts, they fought over what was included as compensation for faculty (e.g., would the cost of salary increases due to normal ongoing promotions be charged to the contract?), and at one point the university had miscalculated part of its own offer.

Table 9.1
Comparing the cases

Ignoring rituals (IH)		Traditional negotiations	
Front stage	Backstage	Front stage	Backstage
Drama of conflict	—	Drama of conflict	**Lead bargainers** work together ↓ Don't take it personally Be honest Be creative Help each other perform well

Moving Integrative Bargaining to the Front Stage

Integrative bargaining is not new to labor negotiations; Walton and McKersie (1965) saw long ago that some integrative bargaining occurs in most negotiations. But it occurs to a limited degree and, I have argued, it tends to occur in backstage settings; it is there that lead bargainers have been able to identify interests, invent options without commitment, and deal with people on a personal level despite their roles as opponents. What MGB training tries to do is to expand the domain of integrative bargaining beyond the backstage.

In some ways the approach to change is similar to what we saw happen at NBP in chapter 7: More people were included in the discussion, oppositional patterns of interaction were dropped, and leadership was broad and shared. But the changes at NBP were secret: The kind of openness that developed among negotiators was hidden from view and traditional external appearances were maintained. They negotiated differently but still engaged in much of the expected drama. And the changes at NBP were emergent rather than planned.

Manage around roles (NBP)		Reshaping rituals (MU)	
Front stage	Backstage	Front stage	Backstage
Drama of conflict	**Both teams** work together	**Both teams** work together	—
	↓	↓	
	Don't take it personally	Don't take it personally	
	Be honest	Be honest	
	Be creative	Be creative	
	Help each other perform well		

At Midwestern, by contrast, the move toward open discussion, problem solving, and inclusion was consciously made. There was no need to keep the process hidden or backstage—the negotiators had a means of accounting[7] for their behaviors: They were generating "interests," inventing "options," and developing "objective criteria" for evaluating ideas. The language of MGB enabled them to explain to constituents why they were acting differently and to reassure them that the changes were beneficial. Negotiators achieved (partially, at least) what Walton and McKersie (1965) thought was impossible: to modify constituents' behavioral expectations.[8]

---

7. Scott and Lyman (1968) argue that when people violate expectations, it is essential that they provide an explanation or account for their action. This reassures the other party that the action was not taken with the intention of hurting or slighting them, which might otherwise be the interpretation given to the action. In the case of changes of bargaining tactics, the existence of a model such as MGB allows bargainers to say that they are acting in unusual ways, not because they personally chose to do so but because these are the actions prescribed by the model that had been agreed upon.

8. They argue: "In actual fact, the behavioral expectations of the primary group become so important that it is very difficult for a negotiator to manipulate them within the context of a given negotiations" (p. 305).

MGB also gave negotiators a model that defined a new set of rituals and a new process. Their actions were no longer governed totally by others' expectations and by the experience of the lead bargainers. The kind of behaviors that had been kept backstage were now formalized and made into a new script for the front stage. This shift reshaped their roles as bargainers and created new rituals for interaction. Negotiators had changed the process, not by ignoring or managing around roles and rituals, but by reshaping the public drama itself. The three cases studied so far in part II are compared in table 9.1.

At Midwestern, MGB did (despite its natural limits) help reshape negotiators' roles and the rituals they enacted. But this intervention was conducted under ideal circumstances: The staff was chosen with MGB in mind, the negotiators were highly educated and comfortable spinning off lots of ideas (if anything, they were more comfortable with generating ideas than with making decisions), and the two sides operated as independent units rather than as a part of multisite negotiations where others controlled their policies and strategies. In many other cases MGB has failed to change the process in significant ways. In the next chapter two additional cases are presented where negotiators were trained in MGB but the process was not used. What worked at Midwestern was not MGB but the use of MGB in a situation where structural changes were already underway. In cases where the social structure of bargaining is not already changed and negotiators' needs for control are not mitigated in some way, it is extremely difficult to redefine the rituals of bargaining.

10

Rejecting Mutual Gains Bargaining: Texas Bell and Western Technologies

Mutual Gains Bargaining (MGB) offers an alternative model for how to negotiate, and did help negotiators at Midwestern to redefine their roles and the rituals of bargaining. Yet in other cases MGB has failed to effectively change the negotiation process. Two such cases are presented in this chapter. At Texas Bell and Western Technologies, both of which were part of the of the Harvard Program on Negotiation project that provided the training for Midwestern University, MGB was tried but was not effectively implemented. In these cases, unlike Midwestern, MGB was not introduced under ideal circumstances: Teams were staffed with established negotiating pros, they had to deal with larger and more active constituent groups, they were not already committed to a cooperative approach to labor-management relations, and there was a high degree of mistrust between labor and management negotiators. In these cases negotiators tried to shift to a new process without being willing to reshape the roles they played or changing the expectations of constituents. Lead bargainers, especially, were not willing to give up the kind of control that comes with the traditional rituals of bargaining.

Texas Bell

In the previous round of negotiations at Texas Bell, there had been a bitter four-day strike. Union representatives felt that they were "beaten" by the company and that, after negotiations, the company implemented policies (regarding health care and profit sharing) that were different from the agreement. Company negotiators, by contrast, thought that the union "wasn't listening": It was the union's job to ask questions and be sure it understood the offer. These negotiations resulted in widespread distrust and a desire by all to find a more effective way to negotiate. Negotiations would be different next time—either more cooperative or more adversarial—but certainly not the same.

When the company's director of human resources heard about the Department of Labor project, he agreed to use MGB in the upcoming negotiations.

Training

The training at Texas Bell was similar to Midwestern's but included more meetings over a longer period of time. The first round of training occurred almost a year before negotiations and included about 45 representatives from each side. The second round, six months later, included only the bargainers and involved an extended, in-depth bargaining simulation. Five months later, they had one day of training as a refresher just prior to bargaining.

These negotiators faced some of the same issues that negotiators at Midwestern had: The distinction between interests and positions was unclear, and any serious attempt to create options and evaluate them objectively would require extensive, ongoing data analysis, as well as repeated conferences with local union officials from around the state. The union did not have enough staff researchers to conduct spontaneous analyses of many options (especially since the holding company had forced the union to bargain in each state separately), and it could not afford additional statewide meetings of local leaders.

In addition these negotiators faced other constraints. First, they were affected by outside parties far more than at Midwestern. Negotiators on each side at Texas Bell were part of a larger bureaucracy: The company's managers reported to executives at the holding company, and the union's negotiators reported to their regional executives. Their actions were constrained by the multistate bargaining strategies of those above them. The union also had to face several dozen independently elected local leaders within the state. There was a much larger, more active, more political, and more influential set of constituents here than at Midwestern.

Second, negotiators at Texas Bell were more experienced than those at Midwestern; they understood and believed in the existing negotiating rules. While younger negotiators thought that MGB made sense, many of the older ones resisted. Especially persistent was the expectation that simply talking about an idea was a signal of commitment to that idea. Therefore several union negotiators did not want in any way to discuss topics such as merit pay: "Why respond to an issue if, by talking about it, they would think we were nibbling at it," explained one top union official.

Third, many of the negotiators had been part of the previous negotiations (or an even more recent, unsuccessful between-contract negotiation over job assignments). As a result their frustration with past negotiations carried over. Discussions during training evolved into arguments about previous negotiations and the union's sense that "agreements made were not agreements kept." From the point of view of many union negotiators, the company had no credibility or integrity. It became impossible to discuss MGB without first examining misunderstandings

that had occurred before and acknowledging, at least, the result-
ing feelings of anger and mistrust.[1] Surveys revealed that union
mistrust of the company had a strong negative impact on their
interest in using MGB and remained strong throughout the
negotiations (Friedman 1993a).

Fourth, at Texas Bell the lead bargainers wanted to maintain
tight control over their teams throughout the training process as
well as the negotiations. The company's lead bargainer demanded that the simulation be rewritten several times so that it would
not be too real. Negotiators on both sides were carefully briefed
on what they could say during the simulations, and the lead bargainers refused to allow their teams to switch roles (switching
roles would encourage their teams to see the other side's point
of view and would somehow, they thought, cause them to reveal
bargaining secrets). Later, during the negotiations, top negotiators imposed strict limits on what could be said and done both
in subcommittee and main-table meetings.

For all of these reasons the level of resistance to MGB at Texas
Bell was high. When a trainer suggested that they bring at least
two options to the table for each issue (in order not to get committed to any position too soon), a union negotiator responded,
"Why spend all that time on new options, working your fanny
off and getting hopes up for a good deal, then get to the end and
the idea disappears?" MGB survived this resistance because
negotiators created a distinction that helped them feel secure—
that between "prebargaining" and "bargaining." A manager
explained, "In *negotiations*, I understand that you have to be
careful about what you say. I was talking about *pre*bargaining."
At this point both sides saw the new process as something that

---

1. The trainer encouraged negotiators to establish ground rules that would protect
them from misunderstandings in the future. Some suggestions that negotiators made
included (1) be clear who can commit, (2) have an end-product review, and (3)
impose check points to make sure that people are seeing the same thing.

would *not* occur during negotiations but prior to the beginning of negotiations.

Prebargaining

Negotiations began with three months of "prebargaining" com-mittee meetings. Negotiators from both sides (except the lead bargainers) divided into four teams covering different topics. Each team, by necessity, had to develop its understanding of mutual gains bargaining and decide how they would conduct themselves. In one group, they agreed on the first day that "if you entertain our off-the-wall BS, we'll entertain your off-the-wall BS." A few months later many negotiators (especially those in two subcommittees that worked very well) talked about feel-ing comfortable with each other, being less adversarial, and building trust among team members. A union bargainer argued that they came to appreciate each other's views, adding, "We opened their eyes to a lot of things that they never knew were going on." And a manager thought that prebargaining allowed them to "get the issues out on the table."

Others, however, were more frustrated with the subcommit-tee phase. One union negotiator said, "I did not understand the process. We did not have a good feeling for what was an interest and what was a position. It seemed so clear when you guys [the trainers] did it." A manager commented, "The union—and to some extent us—proposed positions and called them interests." Another union negotiator felt that the company had "made up their minds six months ago what would happen":

Nothing I said made any impact. It was mechanical. They had speeches, dialogue prepared. We were honest, from the gut. I'd say, "Are we gonna go through another show-and-tell? Let's just talk."

Meanwhile, managers criticized the union for speaking too much "from the gut": their ideas were "not well thought out" and "would have bankrupted the company," according to one manager. And some negotiators learned that their more experienced colleagues did not want discussions to be too open after all. One company bargainer was admonished by a senior colleague for simply agreeing with some criticisms of the company made by a union negotiator.

Even in those cases where the subcommittees did work well, negotiators felt limited by the lead bargainers. One company negotiator saw their strict directives from the lead bargainers as "impediments" to brainstorming. Negotiators also complained that lead bargainers did not build relationships with the other side or work to create an understanding of the mutual gains process, as they did. One company negotiator said:

> The lead bargainers were win-lose. I could see it in how they talked in meetings. When someone takes a cheap shot at someone in the union that you worked with, you get angry.

Another negotiator who heard "disparaging remarks" about the union thought that the lead bargainers were not "part of the process." Apparently some of the lead bargainers, who were not part of the subcommittee meetings, continued to engage in traditional conversations of difference.

Negotiators on all subcommittees were frustrated that they could not accomplish much in these meetings. During this pre-bargaining phase, management was under strict orders not to "negotiate." In the words of the lead bargainer, they could discuss only goals, interests, and options. Later, when formal negotiations began, management allowed subcommittees to make temporary agreements, but when the first one was made, top union leaders put an end to the practice. Unable to accomplish anything substantive, subcommittee teams felt that they were "watching water freeze," as one manager put it. A union negotiator thought that the negotiators from both sides came to know each other well during their subcommittee work, "but everyone was afraid to move."

Some subcommittees came out of this stage with new ideas and a strong sense of loyalty among its members; others ended in frustration. A union negotiator from one of the latter groups said "mutual gains will end on July 5—after July 5, we'll stop this BS."

Main-Table Bargaining

On July 5, the teams reported back to the main table, and formal negotiations began. During July most meetings were still in sub-committees. In the first week of August, subcommittee meetings ended, main-table bargaining began, and offers were made. At this point the top-level negotiators overtly took control; the union's lead bargainer told his team, "No one talks at the table without being called on." These meetings were described as "very formal"; they were used only to make offers and, as one manager put it, to "announce" each side's "collective thoughts." Real bargaining occurred only among a small group of top nego-tiators who met informally, and financial discussions occurred only between the lead bargainers (a few others attended at times). As each higher level of personnel took control, negotia-tions became more private and distant from those who had worked together in subcommittee and tried to use a mutual gains approach. One manager, who had expected to actually negotiate as a result of the MGB training, explained:

I didn't negotiate bullshit. [The top guys] negotiated. I talked and explained positions. We did not sit down with the other side and say, "Let's take care of this or that," because we all knew the rules: "first final offer" and all that. We laughed about it. There was an "offer," a "comprehensive offer," and on Saturday, it was going to be our "final offer"—it was all planned.

Another manager, new to negotiations, said he had learned that there were "unwritten rules about negotiations": "You have to settle in the middle of the night; you can make the decision at 2

PM but the media coverage is not as good." With the MGB approach, this manager added, "You're better prepared," but you still have to follow old rules: "You still have to do all the trading at the last hours." Negotiators continued to perform a drama of conflict for outside audiences, and most substantive discussions occurred backstage between the lead bargainers.

On August 12, the contract expired and the union went on strike. There were no further main-table meetings until the top negotiators reached an agreement. During this time the parent company took greater control of the negotiations. It required, for example, that Texas Bell send a letter to employees explaining the final offer, even though Texas Bell managers thought that this would just antagonize the union. Similarly the union's actions in Texas were constrained by the International's strategy of creating de facto regional bargaining; it wanted Texas to hold out until negotiations in neighboring states were complete. The final agreement was explained to the full negotiating teams at a main-table meeting held throughout the night on August 30.

This package included both base wage increases and lump-sum bonuses, greater flexibility in scheduling excused work days and vacations, no major changes in medical benefits, and an "Options" plan that allowed workers to trade income for more time off. The company accomplished its goal of phasing out a short workweek at some locations, combining some pay bands, and expanding the work that its lowest-level workers would be allowed to do. The union had some problems getting members to accept this contract because the changes benefited some groups more than others, and because the union had built up members' expectations prior to bargaining.[2] In the end the contract was ratified.

---

2. During an extensive "mobilization" effort the union rallied against lump-sum payments and insisted that the company reinstate COLA payments.

The Role of MGB

The MGB process played an important role in these negotiations, but it was only used in prebargaining, not in formal bargaining, and it was used by negotiators in subcommittees, not (publicly, at least) by the top negotiators. Even in subcommittee meetings there was a great deal of confusion about what the subcommittees were allowed to accomplish, and "old hands" brought old habits and constraints into the process. Most saw the MGB process as a good way to build relationships and *prepare* for bargaining. A few managers and union leaders saw it as a clever way to dupe the union.

Negotiators from both sides felt that the MGB process helped them get to know the issues better and their importance to each side. One manager said that MGB "set up a process to share what is important to you." Some results, such as the Options plan, the new idea of a "technological leader," and the shift to a predominantly 40-hour workweek, "could not have happened without an understanding of the problems before negotiations," added another manager. In the end managers thought that the union had a better understanding of the offer than in the past. More broadly, managers felt that they finished negotiations as friends with the union, not enemies, and it seemed that the union was happy with the contract. Employee support for the union was not damaged by these negotiations, as it had been before, and the company continued to work with the union in joint committees after negotiations ended. These positive feelings were more prevalent on the company side than on the union side, and more prevalent among top-level negotiators on both sides than among lower-level negotiators.

Some experienced bitter disappointment. One union negotiator, who "believed in the process, heart and soul," according to his colleague, felt hurt by the collapse of the MGB process. He ended the negotiations saying, "I have no intention of being civil." Another union negotiator thought that "the process began to work, then we all reverted to the jerks we all can be." And some union negotiators felt that they were "outfoxed" by the MGB approach:

It hurt us. We got real chummy. Everyone talked. Then, in the final hours, it was the same old shit. Maybe we should have been pounding on the table. If everyone had played fair, did [MGB], we would have done better. It's too bad. I think eventually the [MGB] type has to replace the old way. The strike is not the answer, especially at this company.

Western Technologies[3]

Negotiators at a Western Technologies parts plant were asked to consider using MGB by one of the trainers who had contacts with the company. The union representatives were skeptical at first, and agreed to try MGB only after meeting with management, hearing trainers explain the ideas, trying the process in simulations, and airing complaints they had about management and what had happened in the last negotiations. Even then, on several occasions, they announced that they would back out of the project. One union negotiator said, prior to training, "I don't see anything wrong with the present system."

The previous round of negotiations had not gone well for the union. It had accepted lump-sum payments with the understanding that the company could not afford base-wage increases for anyone. But after the negotiations, managers received base-wage increases. To make matters worse, the union was angry that retiring workers were not given a pro-rated portion of their lump-sum payment if they left before the scheduled payment date. This seemed especially wrong given that the lump-sum

---

3. The initial write-up of this case was done by Caitlin Deinard, who also observed all of the negotiations. Larry Hunter conducted early interviews of participants and provided information about the history of the relationship between the two sides and their perceptions about the previous round of negotiations.

payments were labeled "service premiums." This situation put great pressure on the union politically, generated strong feelings of distrust, and made people feel that, as one union leader put it, "you have to watch your wording on everything" in negotiations.

The company blamed these problems on the union's lack of preparation and expertise. One manager said, "They have no training in this, they're only elected due to a popularity contest. We have a big advantage in the negotiation. Our preparation is enormous just in the area of pure research." Union negotiators did, in fact, feel overwhelmed by the company's use of data and its capacity to do research, but they were also skeptical of the company's data and felt insulted by the process. One negotiator explained:

> They give us all these movies, slides, the whole works—the cost of health care, a million wage comparisons. It felt like a putdown, the whole thing did. I felt that they were well prepared, while we could not counterattack. I felt as though all the comparisons and stuff were taken out of context. You know, statistics like that can be used in such a way that they don't really tell the truth. Maybe we should do that too. But it would take days, weeks, to match what they do. It's like they have unlimited resources to put all that together. What can we do?

This negotiator hoped that the training would teach the company to "stop beating around the bush" with these presentations.

The key issues in the upcoming negotiations were to be health care and wages. Both sides were also somewhat concerned about work rules, especially limits to worker mobility between jobs: the company wanted greater stability in job assignments, while the union wanted freedom of opportunity for workers. Finally, management wanted (and was required by the government to implement) a total quality management (TQM) program and hoped that the joint training would help to put this program into place.

Training

The first introductory day of training dealt with more than just the ideas of MGB—it also became an opportunity for the two sides to talk about their understanding of what happened in the last round of negotiations. Like at Texas Bell, they could not move forward without dealing with the past. After the company's lead bargainer tried repeatedly to avoid a direct confrontation with the union over the service premium issue from the last negotiations, the trainer asked them to try to clear the air. Management saw the issue as one that could be explained by data on labor-market demands, while the union saw it as a political problem. As one union negotiator put it: "Every day we hear it. 'Why did management not get a service premium?' I hate it. It doesn't matter what was true or who said what. I have to deal with it every day." One union negotiator asked, after learning the basics of MGB, "Are there any steps on how to learn to trust each other?"

The second training session went much smoother than the first. They went through a full-day negotiation simulation and learned about ways in which labor and management could cooperate from a senior union official who had been part of earlier efforts to bring Quality of Work Life innovations into labor relations. These negotiators, like those in other cases, struggled with the MGB ideas. Most negotiators thought that MGB meant compromising more quickly, saying repeatedly "I want to cooperate with you," or simply trying harder in caucuses to come up with packages that the other side would accept. These negotiators usually failed to explain their interests to the other side, they did not allow themselves to consider multiple options for solving problems, and they tended to focus only on areas of "common interest" while avoiding areas where interests conflicted.

Yet a few negotiators on each side did quite well at understanding the MGB approach and became excited about the possibility of using it in practice. Most negotiators agreed that it would be worth trying MGB in the upcoming negotiations. A Federal Mediation and Conciliation Service mediator, Dick Flaherty, volunteered to be available throughout the negotiations as a "process" consultant. And the two sides agreed to explore the possibility of developing a total quality program.

The Negotiations

Between the time when training ended and negotiations began, the International union assigned a staff member to lead the negotiations who had not been part of the training and did not know the people at the company. This event was expected, given the early retirement of the usual negotiator for the union, but it did make the MGB process much harder to implement. When the lead bargainers met for their first planning meetings, Steve Hayes, the newly assigned rep, began to express his concerns about the MGB process. He cautioned that internalizing the principles of MGB would take a lot of time, trust, and credibility, and raised an issue of more immediate and practical concern: Could the union present its list of proposals when negotiations began? Even though the list was a set of positions, not interests, the membership expected their requests to be presented. One company negotiator acknowledged that the union had an underlying interest in the stability of its membership and therefore suggested that they let the union present its list of proposals in order to satisfy members, then go back to derive the interests behind those proposals. Negotiators were struggling with the practical implications of their decision to try MGB; Hayes was openly skeptical of the process.

In the next planning meeting with the full committees, union negotiators discussed (mostly among themselves) the question: Should they tell the membership that they were using MGB? Some argued that as long as the committee gained more for members, it was up to them to choose the negotiating strategy. Hayes disagreed, claiming that for MGB to work, the membership had to be more involved and supportive. He explained that the joint quality program at Ford took years to implement. It was apparent at this point that having missed the training, and with management's constant emphasis on developing a "joint quality program," Hayes confused the latter with the MGB process. From his perspective, if the point of MGB was to develop joint programs, negotiations were not the appropriate time to begin the process. In the end the union negotiators agreed (but for different reasons) that they would not talk with their members about the mutual gains bargaining process.

During this meeting the service premium once again surfaced as an unresolved issue. The union pushed for a promise that management would not propose service premiums again. Tom Burger (the labor relations manager in charge of negotiations while Henders, the vice president of HR, was not there) was angry that the union was trying to limit options; this seemed counter to the whole idea of MGB. The union responded that it was simply reporting a political fact: A contract with service premiums simply could not be ratified. One union negotiator explained that he was being open and honest, as he usually was only in sidebar discussions. Several management negotiators still expressed frustration that the union could not understand the facts that made the service premium necessary last time.

At this meeting negotiators still showed an interest in using the MGB process and were working hard to understand exactly how to implement the new process, but hopes that MGB might actually be used faded when everyone took out their calendars to set the next meeting. Hayes could not meet again for six weeks, and he stated explicitly that with other contracts to negotiate, he could not spend extra time on these negotiations. He worried (accurately) that the new ideas and extra work of MGB would slow down negotiations.

The Opening Days—Struggling to Use MGB

In February, during the first meetings, several efforts were made to use the MGB approach. The company steered the discussion into areas where there was, it thought, some common interest and therefore a chance of reaching agreement. The first item was the use of paid absence allowance (PAA) days. Burger initiated the discussion by saying that he just wanted to talk about ideas and was not expecting to make any commitments. Again, Hayes resisted Burger's efforts, saying that MGB would require too much time, and repeating his earlier argument that this was the wrong place to start implementing "jointness." He responded to each of the ideas that management threw out as if they were formal company proposals that had to be either accepted or rejected. He suggested several times that management should caucus and submit a specific plan for the union's opinion.

Despite Hayes's attempt to cut off MGB, one union negotiator who liked the process, Ed Thomas, asked management negotiators directly what they were trying to achieve with their PAA proposals. Burger answered "lower absenteeism" and "higher productivity." Thomas suggested that in that case, they should separate the PAA issue from the issue of absenteeism: The main cause of absenteeism, he argued, was a "bad atmosphere" between workers and supervisors at the plant. If the company wanted to reduce absenteeism, it should improve relationships. One manager responded that this was an issue that the new quality program might address. Several members of each team participated in this discussion. Periodically Hayes rephrased the points that his team members had made, keeping himself in the middle of the conversation (but just barely) and maintaining some sense that he was still the lead negotiator.

Breaking Away from MGB

Hayes told the mediator, Dick Flaherty, that he still did not think they should be attempting MGB. He worried that lengthy discussions of options would lead some of the committee members to think that they could really achieve the changes that emerged during their brainstorming. As a result, he thought, they would become stuck on minor noneconomic issues, leaving little time for the more important problems that they faced.

According to Flaherty, there was another reason for Hayes's resistance to MGB: As the "new guy on the block" he had yet to establish his authority with this unfamiliar committee. That would be difficult if he was forced to use a bargaining technique that was new to him, was highly unstructured, and for which everyone but himself had received training. Indeed, as Hayes became more familiar with his committee, he took more and more control. In one surprise strategic move, he quickly withdrew several of the union's proposals, putting pressure on the company to do the same. Burger immediately recognized that Hayes was an excellent chess player, who had forced him into following the traditional routine of dropping issues rather than solving problems. Hayes's teammates also grew to respect his bargaining skills during this period, and increasingly felt comfortable letting him direct their strategy.

In the meantime the two sides built up traditional back-door contacts, both through the mediator and through conversations between Burger and the union's local chairman. Burger was quite happy to see Hayes emerge as a leader who was clearly in charge of the union team, and comfortable with the back-door communications that they developed. In caucuses, managers talked more and more about reading the union's signals and asked the mediator to double-check their interpretations. Negotiations were now engaged in the traditional rituals of bargaining, and Flaherty began to play the traditional mediator's role as supporter of private communication between the two sides.

The final nail was put in the MGB coffin when Hayes signed a management proposal and presented it as an agreement. Burger claimed that the proposal was just an idea, that he had only typed it up so that the union would not have to bother with such clerical tasks. Hayes argued that any written proposal was an offer and threatened to take the company to the NLRB for bad-faith bargaining—if Burger had made a mistake in typing up the proposal, that was his problem. Burger responded angrily that he would not make such a mistake again and asked the mediator to tell Hayes that he could do traditional tough-bargaining too. This event, he said, "throws MGB out the window." It had already been several weeks since anyone had mentioned the process.

From here on, negotiations were no different from those in the past. Henders rejoined the negotiations in the final stages, presented all of the financial data that the company had collected, and led the negotiations until the end. He tried to get the union to discuss wages and benefits, but Hayes refused to talk about financial issues until all of the nonfinancial issues were settled. This forced the company to drop most of its nonfinancial requests. Hayes explained to Henders across the table: "I've always bargained this way. I don't want to have to 'buy' a noneconomic piece. I don't want you to 'sell' them." Hayes then agreed to present the union's financial proposals on the second to last day of bargaining. Henders was frustrated that Hayes had effectively cut off all substantive discussion of nonfinancial issues, but respect for Hayes skyrocketed as other managers and his teammates came to see him as a master tactician.

On the last day they met 13 times to make incremental moves on wage proposals and drop or add final pieces of the deal. After they reached an agreement at 11 PM, both sides shook hands and talked informally for a while. In the end workers received base-wage increases, increased pension benefits, COLA was restructured, and there were no changes in the comprehensive health insurance they had. The union committee said that it would recommend the contract, and agreed to jointly explore cost-control measures for health care and develop a total quality program after the negotiations were over. The company allowed the union to use its office resources to create an information booklet to distribute at the ratification meeting, two days later. The contract was passed almost unanimously.

The Role of MGB

In the end the negotiation process at Western Technology was traditional. One young, new member of the union's team said he learned from this experience that "talk is cheap, get it in writing." He was one of the few who was "naive" enough to believe that MGB was "a great idea."

The reality, he found out, was that "It's a poker game in there. I know they're holding back their cards, so why should we risk our three years by showing our cards?" He was happy that Hayes had "gone with what he knew," since "it would have been hard for him to change horses midstream." This negotiator started negotiations believing in the MGB process, yet in the end he was thoroughly socialized into the traditional mode of bargaining. On the positive side, most of the negotiators did feel that this round of negotiations was less acrimonious than before and that the training had helped them air some of their complaints and build a better relationship.

Reshaping Rituals without Reshaping Roles

At Midwestern, the traditional negotiation process was changed to a significant degree, while at Texas Bell and Western Technologies the process remained much more traditional. Providing an alternative model for negotiations—in this case MGB—and training negotiators how to use it is not enough to actually change the process. As long as negotiators want to—or are pressured to—play their traditional roles, the traditional negotiation process will reemerge. This is what occurred at Western Technologies and Texas Bell: Even though there was an attempt to use the MGB process in both cases, top bargainers insisted on retaining their traditional role as leaders and constituent expectations were not changed. As a result the effort to use the MGB process in these negotiations was largely abandoned soon after negotiations began.

In both cases lead bargainer behaviors had a decisive effect on the MGB process: They were not willing to allow their negotiators to stray far from the set agenda, really explore new ideas, or act independently of them. At Western Technologies the union's lead bargainer was new to that bargaining unit and needed to establish himself through his expertise in the traditional bargaining process. While some bargainers were trying to use mutual gains bargaining, he drew them back to the traditional rituals of bargaining to retain his role as lead bargainer. At Texas Bell lead bargainers on both sides sent contradictory signals about their willingness to let their teams implement MGB. On the union side, the lead bargainer was barely convinced that it was worth trying, made sure that the subcommittees that worked in a mutual gains way did not make any deals, and did not let them even talk about some issues, such as merit pay. On the company side, the lead bargainer instructed his negotiators to use MGB, but he kept tight reins on what was said in training simulations and in subcommittee meetings.[4] For both the mutual gains process was allowed to proceed only so far: It was to be used somewhat in "prebargaining," but once they started main-table negotiations, the lead bargainers were totally in control. At Texas Bell and Western Technologies lead bargainers may have talked about using the MGB process but were not willing to allow their own role as lead bargainers to be redefined in any way.

In both cases negotiators also had to deal with a more influential external audience than existed at Midwestern, and one that did not want or was not taught about the MGB process. At Texas Bell both the union and the company's strategies were linked with those of the regional union and the holding company, both of which had ultimate control over negotiations and only grudgingly allowed their bargainers in Texas to use MGB. The union bargainer at Western, as well, reported to the International, not the local. And at both companies union members were angry about the results of the last negotiations; the union's credibility was on the line and members were watching. This was not an opportune time to tell union members that their negotiators would be more cooperative with the company, or to overtly break from their role as conduits of constituent views. Rather it was a time to rally members, tell them what the union would achieve for them, and direct their frustrations at the company. In neither case did the union do much to advertise that they were using a new process or try to change constituent expectations. Moreover, the union still depended on member mobilization for

---

4. As one indicator of the contradictory nature of the lead bargainer's support for MGB, a manager asked a union negotiator in subcommittee if he would do him a "political favor" and agree to put out a joint statement of mutual gains—the lead bargainer had demanded that all subcommittees produce such a document. This lead bargainer wanted his negotiators to use MGB but, ironically, was very *positional* in his understanding of what the results of MGB would be.

leverage; without other sources of leverage or a significant degree of trust in management—absent in both cases—it made more sense to maintain or even enhance traditional expectations among constituents, and play out the drama of conflict.

At Midwestern, by contrast, the new process was widely known and expected by constituents: They voted on using MGB, many of them were part of training, reports from the table explained the MGB process during negotiations, and the language of MGB was used in meetings with the union's board, its bargaining council, and the university's president.[5] And the lead bargainers were not negotiating pros, did not know the traditional bargaining roles, and did not dominate the negotiations. Without these freedoms, negotiators at Texas Bell and Western Technologies were unable to create an atmosphere where they could trust each other, come together as a united group, and focus on solving problems rather than acting out their roles as opponents. With traditional roles and expectations intact, MGB was used very little and, even then, only in ways that would not be visible to constituents (much like NBP, described in chapter 7).

Whither MGB?

As one of the few consciously elaborated alternatives to traditional bargaining, MGB is now being widely talked about in labor-relations circles, sometimes in quite glowing terms but also with a great deal of doubt, cynicism, and even fear (Horvitz 1993; Heckscher 1993; Hunter and McKersie 1992; Friedman 1993b). The approach is hotly debated, and the debates have been made somewhat confusing by the fact that the techniques used to explain MGB, the types of training methods used, and

---

5. Hirsch (1986) has shown that linguistic framing is critical for generating new "rules of the game." It helps to routinize and legitimize a new pattern, and helps participants by making the experience comprehensible and providing a framework for evaluating that experience.

the ways in which the process is implemented during negotiations vary a great deal; any number of consultants have their
own best way to do MGB, can provide examples of glowing success, and can cite examples where others have bungled the job.
From *these* cases it is clear that MGB is difficult to implement:
The distinction between interests and positions is hard to grasp,
the process is often abandoned when it comes time to negotiate
financial issues, there may not be the time and resources (especially for the union) to do as much analysis as demanded by
MGB, and when the process is actually used negotiators often
create ideas faster than constituents can absorb them. These difficulties, however, can be managed and overcome, as we saw in
the Midwestern case.

More damning is the fact that MGB is a process model that
does not change the role structure of labor negotiations, build
trust between the parties, or change the union's dependence on
mobilization for power. In cases like Midwestern, where there
are ongoing efforts to improve the labor management relationship, constituents are hoping for a change, new people are
assigned to negotiate, leadership is shared, and the union can
establish a safety net of an early settlement date, MGB training
can change the rituals of bargaining. But as long as negotiators
face expectations from constituents, lead bargainers, and teammates to enact their traditional roles, the process is not likely to
change. And as long as union negotiators distrust management
and feel powerless without mass mobilization, they will not
abandon the drama of conflict. It is exactly these cases—where
negotiations are already most difficult—that MGB is least likely
to work. There may still be some beneficial side effects of MGB
training in these cases—negotiators may get to know each other
better and have time to discuss issues prior to the actual negotiations—but it is unlikely to significantly alter the traditional rituals of bargaining.

11

The Logic and
Limits of Change

In all of the negotiations studied in part II there was some degree of explicit or implied dissatisfaction with the status quo. For some, the personal costs of months of conflict was too high, and any opportunity for dealing in a less antagonistic way across the table was worth trying. For some, there was a visceral dislike of "playing games" and a desire to make the process more "rational." For some, there was a sense that the old process could not produce innovative solutions to complex problems. And for some, there was a desire to avoid the negative effects on the relationship between labor and management that can come from the drama of conflict. In other words, there were good reasons—ones that mirror the flaws identified in chapter 6—for negotiators to want to change the process.

Many of the desired benefits of change were achieved. At NBP negotiators discussed issues more openly and honestly, and felt good about their involvement in the negotiations. At Midwestern negotiators were able to keep their current health care plan by discovering ways to keep costs down, and the faculty and the administration learned a great deal about the problems that each faced. Even at Texas Bell and Western Technologies there were helpful discussions prior to the negotiations about their relationship as well as some key issues. To

some degree in all four cases, conflict between opposing negotiators was reduced, there was a greater emphasis on the integrative dimension of bargaining, and many participants were
more satisfied with the negotiations.

But these cases also show the limits of change and the difficulty negotiators face tinkering with a complex social system. At
IH efforts to make the system more "rational" and discard the
rituals of bargaining eliminated backstage contacts and heightened the drama of conflict. Efforts to expand the backstage by
keeping outside constituents at bay hurt the credibility of negotiators at NBP. And negotiators at Western Technologies and
Texas Bell were simply unwilling to weaken lead bargainer
dominance or drop public displays of conflict. Even at
Midwestern negotiators had to constantly battle with constituents who were not ready to accept some aspects of the MGB
process. Change can be politically, personally, and organization-
ally costly.

As long as the traditional roles are in place, negotiations
depend on the balance of backstage and front-stage work that is
achieved with the traditional process (see figure 11.1). Negotiators need to be able to publicly show their opposition to the
other side, intrateam unity, and loyalty to constituents, while
privately sharing information, generating ideas, and making
deals. This allows them to meet contradictory role demands of
different audiences, while creating a social space for doing both
integrative and distributive bargaining. The dramatic structure

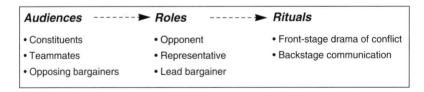

Figure 11.1
Elements of the labor negotiations system

of the traditional bargaining process helps negotiators solve the well-known bargainers "dilemma" of doing both integrative and distributive bargaining (Pruitt and Lewis 1977; Walton and McKersie 1965; Lax and Sebenius 1986),[1] and it helps them to maintain a consistent performance and stay in role. Any far-reaching effort to change the traditional process in a way that eliminates either the front-stage drama or backstage contacts risks destroying this balance.

The most that can be hoped for (barring dramatic changes in the social structure of negotiations and the balance of power between the two sides) is to pull and tug a bit on the dimensions of the old system. It is reasonable to want to expand somewhat the integrative dimensions of bargaining and backstage process-es, while diminishing somewhat the emphasis on distributive bargaining and public conflict; this is what was done at NBP and the mutual gains cases. But how far this can go is limited by tra-ditional role expectations, natural group dynamics concerning group cohesion and leadership, the union's dependence on mobilization for power, and, ultimately, the existence of issues that are inherently distributive. Negotiators can do negotiations in a way that is somewhat more integrative and more like the traditional sidebar meetings between lead bargainers, but they usually cannot (and would not want to) drop all expressions of conflict or use only integrative tactics.

Reexamining the Case for Change

Given the costs of change, we need to return to the question: Is change really necessary? There is much to be criticized about the traditional process, but are we sure that the most commonly

---

1. As Pruitt and Lewis (1977) point out, two other solutions to this dilemma are hav-ing different people do the integrative and distributive bargaining or having the same people do each at different times. The existence of front and backstages allows the same people to do both parts of the negotiations (i.e., the lead bargainers), and it allows negotiators to do them at the same time.

touted alternative,[2] integrative bargaining, is really able to produce better results? Integrative bargaining, based on MGB or
other approaches, addresses many of the problems of traditional
bargaining: excessive conflict, lack of negotiator involvement, a
high potential for misunderstanding, and difficulty finding creative alternatives. And many of behaviors encouraged by those
who seek a more integrative style of bargaining—such as carefully analyzing one's own priorities, exchanging information
about one's most important goals, trying to accurately perceive
the other's priorities, and trying not to personalize the negotiation process—have produced larger joint gains in experimental
research (Rubin and Brown 1975; Pruitt and Lewis 1977). Still
there is no evidence from the field that interventions like MGB
produce better results.

In the MGB cases studied here, some of the more important or
innovative outcomes—such as the Options plan at Texas Bell or
the commitment to develop a quality program at Western
Technologies—were not the result of MGB but of management's
insistence that they be included. It may be that MGB took
enough of the edge off of negotiations to make the union feel
comfortable saying "yes" to these requests, but they were not
ideas generated through joint brainstorming and problem-solving during negotiations. Even where agreements did come more
directly from MGB-inspired brainstorming and problem-solving,
we can not know if negotiators might have found those solutions without MGB.[3] More broadly, except for a few identifiable

---

2. Companies might consider exiting from the bargaining relationship as another
alternative. This is being done, and options of this type have been described as one
element of the meta negotiations that labor and management engage in concerning
the overall state of their relationship (see Walton, Cutcher-Gershenfeld, and
McKersie, forthcoming), but it does not represent a change in how people negotiate.
Rather, it represents an end to negotiations.
3. Some very innovative agreements have come out of the traditional process done
well. One case where the traditional system was used to great effect is the negotiations between Ford and the UAW in 1982. Based largely on the relationship of trust
between the union's lead bargainer Don Ephlin and the company's lead bargainer

good ideas, most of the results of these or any negotiations are hard to judge and compare in any objective way.[4] Was it better that the parties ended up at 5% rather than 4% or 6%? And many of the more important factors are highly qualitative and difficult to assess. Was the relationship between the two sides improved, or at least not made worse from the negotiations? Did the final agreement help ensure the survival of the company, and of the union? On a more personal level, did individuals feel accepted by their team, competent in their abilities, and involved in the negotiations? Like constituents judging their negotiators, it is hard for us to know if the results from any particular attempt to make negotiations more integrative produced better results.

While there is no concrete evidence that interventions such as MGB produce better results than the traditional process, nor even any reasonable way to make such a comparison, four *logical* arguments can be made for an increased emphasis on integrative bargaining in some labor negotiations. First, where competitive pressures on businesses have increased significantly, even small improvements may be critically important. If integrative bargaining can help the parties discover just one idea that is marginally better, that improvement may be enough to make a difference (even though too small to pick up clearly in large-scale research). Second, in those cases where organizations need to develop greater cooperation with employees (e.g., to enhance quality and productivity), those efforts are hard to sustain if the negotiation process heightens conflict and destroys trust between the two sides. Whether or not integrative bargaining

---

Pete Pestillo, the negotiations produced a contract that included profit sharing and job security guarantees in return for a wage freeze and delays in COLA payments, and created mutual growth forums to improve communication between the company and the union at the local level.
4. Analytically we would like to know if these negotiators found all possible joint gains (the results would then be "Pareto optimal"). But outside of carefully crafted bargaining games or simulations, it is hard to know if any particular agreement did or did not leave potential joint gains on the table.

improves the quality of the immediate negotiating outcome, any change that minimizes public conflicts may still be useful if it ensures that the negotiations do not disrupt other labor-management initiatives.

Third, what may be most critical is not the effect of integrative bargaining on the average negotiation but rather the ability of the process to handle negotiations where nonincremental changes are needed. Those industries that are facing significant, nonmarginal changes in their operations need to find ways to discover new, unknown, and nonobvious solutions to how their people are managed and how their work is organized. Integrative bargaining may increase the chance that very innovative ideas are created, enabling these companies to survive. Finally, there may be cases where the public drama is conducted in a way that precludes backstage work, or where lead bargainers are not able to maintain private communications (e.g., because they are new to the process or each other); they need to emphasize integrative bargaining just to arrive at the balance of integrative and distributive bargaining that makes the traditional system work.

Despite the lack of definitive evidence that interventions designed to create more integrative bargaining produce better outcomes, there are circumstances where managers and labor leaders might sensibly decide that a change in the process would be highly beneficial. In the past—with comfortable profit margins, little competition, and stable union membership—the uncertain benefits of alternatives like MGB might not seem very attractive. For many companies and unions in today's world, that is no longer the case.

Is Change Possible?

The problem that remains however, is the other side of the equation—the costs of change. Negotiators still face powerful forces to stay in their traditional roles, and fear the loss of expertise and control that change might bring. Unions, especially, are loath to abandon rituals that help them mobilize members and provide them with their only base of power. In the cases studied here, there was as much fear of change as there was dissatisfaction with the status quo. MGB training offered an alternative process to negotiators but was unable to eliminate the pressures that created the traditional process in the first place. Any hope that integrative bargaining can be enhanced depends on finding ways to change the role structure of negotiations, not just offering a new process.

One of the best-known cases in recent years where a more integrative approach to negotiations was fully implemented was the 1989 negotiations between Harvard University and its Clerical and Technical Workers' union (HUCTW) following the union's recognition by the university (Hoerr 1993). Both Harvard and HUCTW appointed faculty and staff of the university to negotiate, rather than outside professionals, they split themselves up into eight problem-solving teams (including about 50 university managers and 65 bargaining unit members), and they spent months in exploratory meetings during which the two sides got to know each other well and gathered a great deal of information about the university and its employees. Antimanagement sentiment was not the dominant part of either the union's organizing campaign (they proclaimed: "It is not anti-Harvard to be pro-union") or the negotiations that followed. This example shows what can be done when constituent expectations are different, when the union finds ways to rally members without being antimanagement, when time is spent building trust and a common understanding of problems, and when the basic structure of the negotiating team is allowed to vary.

But the conditions that made those structural changes possible may be hard to reproduce. If ever there was a lead bargainer who would not have to prove his mettle to constituents and would have the leverage to override their expectations and demands, John Dunlop, the administration's lead bargainer, was it. Dunlop, a former secretary of labor, a personal friend of the university's president, and a luminary in the field of labor relations, had a degree of leverage and skill that is far above what is normal. Moreover, after such an inspiring first round of negotiations at HUCTW, the second round three years later was far more difficult, drawn out, and antagonistic. As negotiations became more routinized and Dunlop was no longer in charge, many of the traditional roles and rituals began to emerge.

Several other, more generic, strategies for change are also being developed that begin to address the problem of social context. One approach is to expand the intervention beyond bargaining—to help the two sides change their overall relationship, build greater acceptance and trust in each other, and redefine the roles of bargainers prior to the start of bargaining (and even prior to the start of training). One trainer (Susskind, Carlson, and Roberts 1993), for example, has begun providing ongoing training in mutual gains (not mutual gains "bargaining") between contract negotiations, as well as during negotiations. Another (Rice et al. 1993) has used MGB as only one piece of a broader process of building trust between labor and management. In both cases the goal is to reduce the degree to which the union feels at risk institutionally (so that it does not need to enact the labor-management conflict during negotiations for political purposes), to focus on constituent expectations early enough to make a difference, and to influence (long before bargaining begins) who is put on the bargaining teams and how the teams are organized. This is an approach I have argued for elsewhere (Friedman 1993a), but such interventions do have their own constraints: They require a great deal of commitment to initiate, and a great deal of effort and money to pull off. The very scope of this approach makes it difficult to implement in many situations.

A second approach is to impose on negotiators a very specific, formally defined, step-by-step process that forces change and does not allow negotiators to act on any traditional role pressures that still exist. One trainer with the National College of Education (Tooredman 1990), for example, requires negotiators to go through a series of ten phases, beginning with a meeting between the college president and the faculty (she works only with schools), moving through several weeks of "protocol discussions" and group "retreats," and ending in contract writing and a "victory party." Another from the Federal Mediation and Conciliation Service (Power 1990) requires each side to engage in a structured issue identification process (using his forms and a computerized data "assembly" system), an issue classification process, and a data compilation and feedback process. Both trainers allow negotiators to make some choices, but much of the process is predetermined and very tightly controlled. This approach has been successful in terms of ensuring that negotiators actually do change how they negotiate but has tended to be viable only with small bargaining units and trainers who are in a position to reject any clients who do not agree to conform to their program; only under such circumstances, it appears, can trainers gain enough leverage to simply impose a different process (Friedman 1992a).

These examples highlight how much is needed to overcome the social structure of labor negotiations—in terms of commitments, resources, and trust—and how unusual the conditions are that make these changes possible. There are few negotiators available with the skill and leverage that Dunlop had during the HUCTW negotiations—most negotiators depend somewhat on the drama of conflict to enact their roles as representatives and leaders. Only in unusual circumstances do trainers have the leverage to strictly impose new behaviors on negotiators the way that Power and Tooredman have done. And trust building between labor and management is made difficult by the weak legal protections that unions have as institutions, the ease with which management can switch to union-busting tactics, and a concern among union leaders that change efforts like MGB are driven by managers' need to appear innovative for their corporate audiences rather than a sincere desire to change.[5]

But these examples also help show the level at which change must occur if there is any hope of transforming the negotiation process. Consistent with the model of negotiations developed in part I, change of behavior depends on mitigating the influence of roles pressures and audience expectations. It requires not just a new process but a shift in the social structure of negotiations, including who is at the table, how they are authorized to be there, what constituents expect, and how negotiating teams are formed and led. Absent these efforts, attempts to break out of the traditional rituals of negotiation are likely to be overwhelmed by the social logic that created those rituals in the first place. Changing negotiating behavior requires more than just changes in the negotiating script—it requires changes in the dramatic structure of labor negotiations.

---

5. A recent book has pointed out management's obsession with newness: "As leading management guru Tom Peters bluntly put it, the answer for organizations is simple: 'Get innovative or get dead.' For managers who have taken his message at face value, the quest for new organizational practices—for new words, new structures, new designs, new systems, and new strategies—has become a rather frenzied pursuit" (Eccles and Nohria 1992, 4).

References

Abercrombie, Nicholas, Stephen Hill, and Bryan S. Turner. 1984. *Dictionary of Sociology*. New York: Penguin.

Adams, J. Stacy. 1976. The structure and dynamics of behavior in organizational boundary roles. In *Handbook of Industrial and Organizational Psychology*. Chicago: Rand–McNally, pp. 1175–1199.

Andrews, Kenneth R. 1980. *The Concept of Corporate Strategy*. Homewood, IL: Irwin.

Axelrod, Robert. 1984. *The Evolution of Cooperation*. New York: Basic Books.

Bacharach, Samuel B., and Edward J. Lawler. 1988. *Bargaining: Power, Tactics, and Outcomes*. San Francisco: Jossey–Bass.

Bales, Robert F., and Philip E. Slater. 1955. Role differentiation in small decision–making groups. In. *The Family: Socialization and Interaction Processes*, edited by T. Parsons and R. F. Bales et al. Glencoe, IL: Free Press, ch. 5

Bales, Robert F., and Fred L. Strodbeck. 1951. Phases in group problem solving. *Journal of Abnormal and Social Pyschology* 46:485–495.

Barley, Stephen R. 1991. Contextualizing conflict: Notes on the anthropology of dispute and negotiation. In *Handbook of Research on Negotiation*, vol. 3, edited by Max H. Bazerman, Roy J. Lewicki, and Blair H. Sheppard. Greenwich, CT: JAI Press, pp. 165–199.

Bavales, Alex 1950. Communication patterns in task oriented groups. *Journal of the Acoustical Society of America* 22:271–282.

Bazerman, Max H., and Margaret A. Neale. 1992. *Negotiating Rationally*. New York: Free Press.

Berger, Peter L., and Thomas Luckman. 1967. *The Social Construction of Reality*. Garden City, NY: Anchor Books.

Bok, Derek C., and John T. Dunlop. 1970. *Labor and the American Community*. New York: Simon and Schuster.

Bourdieu, Pierre. 1977. *Outline of a Theory of Practice*. Cambridge: Cambridge University Press.

Brown, Roger. 1986. *Social Psychology*. 2d ed. New York: Free Press.

Canning, David. 1989. Bargaining theory. In *The Economics of Missing Market Information and Games*, edited by F. Hahn. Oxford: Oxford University Press, pp. 163–187.

Cherim, Stanley. 1982. From both sides of the bargaining table. *Educational Record* (summer): 14–16.

Collins, Randall. 1975. *Conflict Sociology: Toward an Explanatory Science*. New York: Academic Press.

Cutcher-Gershenfeld, Joel. 1993. Bargaining over how to bargain: Addressing the limitations of interest-based bargaining in labor negotiations. Unpublished manuscript.

Cyert, Richard M., and James G. March. 1963. *A Behavioral Theory of the Firm*. Englewood Cliffs, NJ: Prentice Hall.

DiMaggio, Paul J., and Walter W. Powell. 1983. The Iron cage revisited: Institutional isomorphism and collective rationality in organizational fields. *American Sociological Review* 48(April):147–160.

Dore, Ronald. 1983. Goodwill and the spirit of market capitalism. *British Journal of Sociology* 34(4):459–482.

Dore, Ronald. 1973. *British Factory–Japanese Factory: The Origins of National Diversity in Industrial Relations*. Berkeley: University of California Press.

Douglas, Ann. 1962. *Industrial Peacemaking*. New York: Columbia University Press.

Douglas, Mary. 1986. *How Institutions Think*. Syracuse: Syracuse University Press.

Druckman, Daniel. 1978. Boundary role conflict: Negotiation as dual responsiveness. In *The Negotiation Process: Theories and Application*, edited by I. William Zartman. London: Sage, pp. 87–110.

Dunlop, John T. 1984. *Dispute Resolution: Negotiation and Consensus Building*. Dover, MA: Auburn House.

Dyer, Davis, Malcolm S. Salter, and Alan M. Webber. 1987. *Changing Alliances*. Boston: Harvard Business School Press.

Eccles, Robert G., and Nitin Nohria. 1992. *Beyond the Hype: Rediscovering the Essence of Management*. Boston: Harvard Business School Press.

Edelman, Murray. 1977. *Political Language: Words That Succeed and Policies That Fail*. New York: Academic Press.

Fantasia, Rick. 1988. *Cultures of Solidarity: Consciousness, Action, and Contemporary American Workers*. Berkeley: University of California Press.

Feldman, Martha S., and James G. March. 1981. Information in organizations as signal and symbol. *Administrative Science Quarterly* 26:171–186.

Fiedler, Klaus, Gun R. Semin, and Stefanie Bolten. 1989. Language use and reification of social information: Top–down and bottom–up processing in person cognition. *European Journal of Social Psychology* 19:271–295.

Fiorito, Jack. 1991. Union growth and decline: A research agenda for the 1990's. In *Industrial Relations Research Association Series: Proceedings of the Forty-third Annual Meeting*, edited by John E. Burton, Jr. Madison: IRRA, pp. 284–292.

Fisher, Roger, and William Ury. 1981. *Getting to Yes*. Boston: Houghton Mifflin.

Flanders, Alan. 1972. What are trade unions for? In *Trade Unions: Selected Readings*, edited by W. E. J. McCarthy. Baltimore: Penguin, pp. 17–27.

Follett, Mary Parker. 1942. *Dynamics of Administration: Collected Papers of Mary Parker Follet*, edited by H. C. Metcalf and L. Urwick. New York: Harper and Row.

Frank, Robert H. 1985. *Choosing the Right Pond: Human Behavior and the Quest for Status*. New York: Oxford University Press.

French, John R. P., Jr., and Bertram Raven. 1959. The social bases of power. In *Studies in Social Power*, edited by Dorwin Cartwright. Ann Arbor, MI: Institute for Social Research, University of Michigan.

Friedman, Raymond A. 1993a. Bringing mutual gains bargaining to labor negotiations: The role of trust, understanding, and control. *Human Resource Management Journal* 32(4):435–460.

Friedman, Raymond A. 1993b. Missing ingredients in MGB theory. Presented at Innovations in Negotiation and Grievance Handling in the New Industrial Relations Order. Program on Negotiation, Harvard University, May 20–21.

Friedman, Raymond A. 1992a. From theory to practice: Critical choices for "Mutual Gains" Training. *Negotiation Journal* 8(2):91–98.

Friedman, Raymond A. 1992b. The culture of mediation: Private understandings in the context of public conflict. In *Hidden Conflict: Uncovering Behind-the-Scenes Disputes*, edited by Deborah Kolb and Jean Bartunek. Beverly Hills: Sage.

Friedman, Raymond A. 1989. Interaction norms as carriers of organizational culture: A study of labor negotiations at international harvester. *Journal of Contemporary Ethnography* 18(1):3–29.

Friedman, Raymond A., and Donna Carter. 1993. African-American network groups: Their impact and effectiveness. Washington, DC: Executive Leadership Council.

Friedman, Raymond A., and Caitlin Deinard. 1991. Black caucus groups at Xerox corporation (A). HBS Case Services, No. 9-491-047.

Friedman, Raymond A., and Shahaf Gal. 1991. Managing around roles: Building groups in labor negotiations. *Journal of Applied Behavioral Sciences* 27(3):356–378.

Friedman, Raymond, and Joel Podolny. 1992. Differentiation of boundary spanning roles: Labor negotiations and implications for role conflict. *Administrative Science Quarterly* 37:28–47.

Gambetta, Diego, ed. 1988. *Trust: Making and Breaking Cooperative Relations*. Oxford: Basil Blackwell.

Garfinkel, Harold. 1967. *Studies in Ethnomethodology*. Cambridge: Polity Press.

Geddes, Deanna. 1991. Opponent analysis in caucus negotiation: A cognitive/communication process. Presented at Academy of Management, Miami.

Goetz, Charles J., and Robert E. Scott. 1981. Principles of relational contracts. *Virginia Law Review* 67(6):1089–1150.

Goffman, Erving. 1959. *The Presentation of Self in Everyday Life*. Garden City, NY: Doubleday.

Goldfield, Michael. 1987. *The Decline of Organized Labor in the United States*. Chicago: University of Chicago Press.

Gouldner, Alvin W. 1952. The problem of succession in bureaucracy. In *Reader in Bureaucracy*, edited by R. K. Merton et al. Glencoe, IL: Free Press, pp. 339–351.

Granovetter, Mark S. 1985. Economic action, social structure and embeddedness. *American Journal of Sociology* 91:481–510.

Gray, Barbara. 1989. *Collaborating: Finding Common Ground for Multiparty Problems*. San Francisco: Jossey–Bass.

Gusfield, Joseph R. 1981. *The Culture of Public Problems: Drinking–Driving and the Symbolic Order*. Chicago: University of Chicago Press.

Gusfield, Joseph R. 1963. *Symbolic Crusade: Status Politics and the American Temperance Movement*. Urbana: University of Illinois Press.

Hamermesh, Richard G., and Evelyn T. Christiansen. 1985. International harvester. HBS Case Services. Nos. 9-381-052 through 9-381-056.

Heckscher, Charles. 1993. Searching for mutual gains in labor relations. In *Negotiation: Strategies for Mutual Gain*, edited by Lavinia Hall. Newbury Park, CA: Sage, pp. 86–104.

Heckscher, Charles. 1988. *The New Unionism*. New York: Basic Books.

Hicks, J. R. [1932] 1963. *The Theory of Wages*. 2d ed. New York: St. Martin's Press.

Hirsch, Paul M. 1986. From ambushes to golden parachutes: Corporate takeovers as an instance of cultural framing and institutional integration. *American Journal of Sociology* 91(4):800–837.

Hochschild, Arlie. 1983. *The Managed Heart: Commercialization of Human Feelings*. Berkeley: University of California Press.

Hochschild, Arlie. 1975. The sociology of feeling and emotion. In *Another Voice*, edited by M. Millman and R. M. Kanter. New York: Doubleday.

Hoerr, John. 1993. Solidaritas at Harvard: Organizing in a different voice. *The American Prospect* (summer): 67–82.

Horvitz, Wayne. 1993. "New" labor-management relations: A cautionary tale. Presented at Innovations in Negotiation and Grievance Handling in the New Industrial Relations Order. Program on Negotiation, Harvard University, May 20–21.

Hunter, Larry W., and Robert B. McKersie. 1992. Can "mutual gains" training change labor-management relationships? *Negotiation Journal* 8(4):319–330.

Ikle, Fred Charles. [1964] 1985. *How Nations Negotiate.* New York: Harper and Row. Kraus Reprint.

Jackall, Robert. 1988. *Moral Mazes: The World of Corporate Managers.* Oxford: Oxford University Press.

Kahn, Robert H., Donald M. Wolfe, Robert Quinn, J. Diedrick Snoek, and Robert Rosenthal. 1964. *Organizational Stress: Studies in Role Conflict and Ambiguity.* New York: Wiley.

Katznelson, Ira. 1981. *City Trenches: Urban Politics and the Patterning of Class in the United States.* New York: Pantheon.

Klimoski, Richard J., and Ronald A. Ash. 1974. Accountability and negotiator behavior. *Organizational Behavior and Human Performance* 11:409–425.

Kochan, Thomas A. 1980. *Collective Bargaining and Industrial Relations.* Homewood, IL: Irwin.

Kochan, Thomas A., Harray C. Katz, and Robert B. McKersie. 1986. *The Transformation of American Industrial Relations.* New York: Basic Books.

Kolb, Deborah M. 1985. To be a mediator: Expressive tactics in mediation. *Journal of Social Issues* 41(2):11–26.

Kolb, Deborah M. 1983. *The Mediators.* Cambridge: MIT Press.

Krackhardt, David, Mark Lundberg, and Laura O'Rourke. 1993. KrackPlot: A picture is worth a thousand words. *Connections* 16:37–47

Laumann, Edward O. 1973. *Bonds of Pluralism.* New York: Wiley–Interscience.

Laumann, Edward O., and Peter V. Marsden. 1979. The analysis of oppositional structures in political elites: Identifying collective actors. *American Sociology Review* 44:713–732.

Lax, David A., and James K. Sebenius. 1986. *The Manager as Negotiator.* New York: Free Press.

Leach, Edmund. 1968. Ritual. In *International Encyclopedia of the Social Sciences,* edited by David L. Sills. New York: Macmillian and Free Press, pp. 520–526.

Leif, Harold, and Renee C. Fox. 1963. Training for "detatched concern" in medical students. In *The Psychological Basis of Medical Practice,* edited by H. Lief, V. Lief, and N. Lief. New York: Harper and Row, pp. 12–35.

Lewicki, Roy J., and Joseph A. Litterer. 1985. *Negotiation.* Homewood, IL: Irwin.

Lorenz, Edward H. 1992. Trust and the flexible firm: International comparisons. *Industrial Relations* 31(3):455–472.

Lorsch, Jay, and Gary Loveman. 1991. Human resource management at American Airlines. HBS Case Services, No. N1-491-097.

Luhmann, Niklas. 1979. *Trust and Power: Two Works by Niklas Luhmann*. New York: Wiley.

Macaulay, S. 1963. Non-contractual relations in business. *American Sociological Review* 28:55–70.

Mannix, Elizabeth A. 1993. Organizations as resource dilemmas: The effects of power and balance on coalition formation in small groups. *Organizational Behavior and Human Decision Processes* 55(1):1–22.

March, James G., and Herbert A. Simon. 1958. *Organizations*. Reading, MA: Addison-Wesley.

Marques, Jose M., Vincent Y. Yzerbyt, and Jacques-Philippe Leyens. 1988. The "Black sheep effect": Extremity of judgments toward ingroup members as a function of group identification. *European Journal of Social Psychology* 18(1):1–16.

Marsh, Barbara. 1985. *A Corporate Tragedy: The Agony of International Harvester Company*. New York: Doubleday.

Marsh, Barbara, and Sally Saville. 1982. International harvester's story: How a great company lost its way. *Crain's Chicago Business*, November 8.

McCormick, Janice. 1985. Threatened industries: Can collective bargaining adapt? In *Human Resource Management: Trends and Challenges*, edited by R. E. Walton and P. Lawrence. Boston: Harvard Business School Press, pp. 141–175.

McKersie, Robert. 1991. Governance: A framework for our field, In *Industrial Relations Research Association Series: Proceedings of the Forty–Third Annual Meeting*, edited by H. Burton, Jr. Madison: IRRA, pp. 1–10.

Mead, George Herbert. 1934. *Mind, Self, and Society*. Chicago: University of Chicago Press.

Merry, Sally E., and Susan S. Silbey. 1984. What do plaintiffs want? Reexamining the concept of dispute. *Justice System Journal* 9(2):151–178.

Merton, Robert K. 1957. *Social Theory and Social Structure*. New York: Free Press.

Meyer, John W., and Brian Rowan. 1977. Institutionalized organizations: Formal structure as myth and ceremony. *American Journal of Sociology* 83(3):539–550.

Mills, D. Quinn. 1989. *Labor–Management Relations*. 4th ed. New York: McGraw-Hill.

Murray, Alan I., and Yonatan Reshef. 1988. American Manufacturing Unions' stasis: A paradigmatic perspective. *Academy of Management Review* 13(4):615–626.

Nash, John F. 1950. The bargaining problem. *Econometrica* 18:155–162.

Neale, Margaret A., and Max H. Bazerman. 1991. *Cognition and Rationality in Negotiation*. New York: Free Press.

Nelson, Reed Eliot. 1983. Social networks and organizational intervention: The case of the Jamestown area labor management committee. Ph.D. dissertation. Cornell University.

Olson, Mancur, Jr. 1965. *The Logic of Collective Action: Public Goods and the Theory of Groups*. Cambridge: Harvard University Press.

Parsons, Talcott. 1963. On the concept of influence. *Public Opinion Quarterly* 27:37–62.

Peters, Edward. 1955. *Strategy and Tactics in Labor Negotiations*. New London, CT: National Foremen's Institute.

Power, Don. 1990. Target specific bargaining process. Paper presented at Mutual Gains Bargaining Seminar, Harvard Kennedy School of Government, December 14.

Pruitt, Dean G. 1981. *Negotiation Behavior*. New York: Academic Press.

Pruitt, Dean G. 1971. Indirect communication and the search for agreement in negotiation. *Journal of Applied Social Psychology* 1(3):205–239.

Pruitt, Dean G., and Steven A. Lewis. 1977. The psychology of integrative bargaining, In *Negotiations: Social Psychological Perspectives*, edited by Daniel Druckman. London: Sage, pp. 161–192.

Pruitt, Dean G., and Jeffrey Z. Rubin. 1986. *Social Conflict: Escalation, Stalemate, and Settlement*. New York: Random House.

Purcel, Theodore V. 1954. *The Worker Speaks His Mind: On Company and Union*. Cambridge: Harvard University Press.

Putnam, Robert. 1988. Diplomacy and domestic politics: The logic of two-level games, *International Organization* 42(3):427–460.

Quinn, James B. 1980. *Strategies for Change: Logical Incrementalism*. Homewood, IL: Irwin.

Rice, Thomas, John Sieg, and William Golt (with Charles Heckscher). 1993. Mutual gains in the context of workplace transformation. Presented at Innovations in Negotiation and Grievance Handling in the New Industrial Relations Order. Program on Negotiation, Harvard University, May 20–21.

Robinson, Robert J., Dacher Keltner, A. Ward, and Lee Ross. 1992. Misconstruing the other side: Real and perceived differences in three ideological conflicts. Unpublished manuscript.

Ross, Lee. 1977. The intuitive psychologist and his shortcomings: Distortions in the attribution process. In *Advances in Experimental Social Psychology*, edited by L. Berkowitz. New York: Academic Press, pp. 173–220.

Rubin, Jeffrey Z., and Bert R. Brown. 1975. *The Social Psychology of Bargaining*. New York: Academic Press.

Saunders, Martha Dunagin. 1992. *Eastern's Armageddon: Labor Conflict and the Destruction of Eastern Airlines*. London: Greenwood Press.

Sayles, Leonard R., and George Strauss. 1953. *The Local Union*. New York: Harper and Row.

Schein, Edgar. 1988. *Process Consultation*. Reading, MA: Addison-Wesley.

Schelling, Thomas C. 1960. *The Strategy of Conflict*. Cambridge: Harvard University Press.

Schlenker, Barry R. 1980. *Impression Management: The Self-Concept, Social Identity, and Interpersonal Relations*. Malabar, FL: Krieger Publishing.

Schott, Susan. 1979. Emotion and social life: A symbolic interactionist framework. *American Journal of Sociology* 84(6):1317–1334.

Schudson, Michael. 1986. Memory as a social force. Research proposal.

Schutz, Alfred. 1962. The problems of social reality. In *Collected Papers*, vol. 1, edited with an introduction by Maurice Natanson. The Hague: Nijhoff.

Scott, Marvin B. and Stanford M. Lyman. 1968. Accounts. *American Sociological Review* 33(1):46–61.

Selekman, Benjamin M. 1947. *Labor Relations and Human Relations*. New York: McGraw-Hill.

Semin, G. R., and K. Fiedler. 1989. Relocating attributional phenomena within a language–cognition interface: The case of actors' and observers' perspectives. *European Journal of Social Psychology* 19:491–508.

Sitkin, Sim B., and Nancy L. Roth. 1991. The limited effect of legalistic remedies for distrust: The case of formalized organizational responses to the stigma of HIV/AIDS. Draft paper. March.

Snow, David A., E. Burke Rochford, Jr., Stein K. Worden, and Robert D. Benford. 1986. Frame alignment processes, micromobilization, and movement participation. *American Sociological Review* 51:464–481.

Stouffer, S. A., et al. 1949. *The American Soldier*, vol. 1. Princeton: Princeton University Press.

Strauss, Anselm. 1978. *Negotiations: Varieties, Contexts, Processes, and Social Order*. San Francisco: Jossey-Bass.

Sudnow, David. 1965. Normal crimes: Sociological features of the penal code in a public defender's office. *Social Problems* 12:255–276.

Susskind, Lawrence, and Jeffrey Cruikshank. 1987. *Breaking the Impasse*. New York: Basic Books.

Susskind, Lawrence E., George O. Carlson, and David B. Roberts. 1993. Southern New England Telephone and the Connecticut Union of Telephone Workers. Presented at Innovations in Negotiation and Grievance Handling in the New Industrial Relations Order. Program on Negotiation, Harvard University, May 20–21.

Sutton, Robert I. 1991. Maintaining norms about emotional expression: The case of bill collectors. *Administrative Science Quarterly* 36:245–268.

Tajfel, Henri. 1981. *Human Groups and Social Categories*. Cambridge: Cambridge University Press.

Tooredman, K. J. 1990. Win-win bargaining: Techniques and impact. Paper presented to the Gateway Chapter of the Industrial Relations Research Association, St. Louis, February 20.

Tracy, Lane, and Richard B. Peterson. 1986. A behavioral theory of labor negotiations—How well has it aged? *Negotiation Journal* 2(1):93–108.

Turner, Ralph H. 1975. Rule learning as role learning: What an interactive theory of roles adds to the theory of social norms. *International Journal of Critical Sociology* 1:34–48.

Van Maanen, John. 1988. *Tales of the Field: On Writing Ethnography*. Chicago: University of Chicago Press.

Van Maanen, John, and Gideon Kunda. 1989. Real feelings: Emotional expression and organizational culture. *Research in Organizational Behavior* 11:43–103.

Walton, Richard E., and Robert B. McKersie. 1965. *A Behavioral Theory of Labor Negotiations: An Analysis of a Social Interaction System*. New York: McGraw-Hill.

Walton, Richard E., Joel Cutcher-Gershenfeld, and Robert B. McKersie. *Strategic Negotiations: A Theory of Change in Labor-Management Relations*. Cambridge: Harvard Business School Press, forthcoming.

Weber, Max. 1947. *The Theory of Social and Economic Organization*, edited by A. H. Henderson and Talcott Parsons. Glencoe, IL: Free Press.

Weiler, Paul C. 1990. *Governing the Workplace: The Future of Labor and Employment Law*. Cambridge: Harvard University Press.

Young, Oran R., ed. 1975. *Bargaining: Formal Theories of Negotiation*. Chicago: University of Illinois Press.

Zartman, William I., and Maureen R. Berman. 1982. *The Practical Negotiator*. New Haven: Yale University Press.

Zeuthen, Frederik. 1930. *Problems of Monopoly and Economic Welfare*. London: Routledge.

Zucker, Lynne G. 1986. Production of trust: Institutional sources of economic structure, 1840–1920. *Research in Organizational Behavior* 8:52–111.

Index